Cambridge Elements

Elements in Early Christian Literature
edited by
Garrick V. Allen
University of Glasgow

ORIGEN ON DEMONIC EXECUTIONERS AND THE PROBLEM OF EVIL

Ky Heinze
Our Lady Seat of Wisdom College

Shaftesbury Road, Cambridge CB2 8EA, United Kingdom

One Liberty Plaza, 20th Floor, New York, NY 10006, USA

477 Williamstown Road, Port Melbourne, VIC 3207, Australia

314–321, 3rd Floor, Plot 3, Splendor Forum, Jasola District Centre,
New Delhi – 110025, India

103 Penang Road, #05–06/07, Visioncrest Commercial, Singapore 238467

Cambridge University Press is part of Cambridge University Press & Assessment,
a department of the University of Cambridge.

We share the University's mission to contribute to society through the pursuit of
education, learning and research at the highest international levels of excellence.

www.cambridge.org
Information on this title: www.cambridge.org/9781009543712
DOI: 10.1017/9781009543750

© Ky Heinze 2026

This publication is in copyright. Subject to statutory exception and to
the provisions of relevant collective licensing agreements, no reproduction
of any part may take place without the written permission of
Cambridge University Press & Assessment.

When citing this work, please include a reference to the
DOI 10.1017/9781009543750

First published 2026

A catalogue record for this publication is available from the British Library

*A Cataloging-in-Publication data record for this Element is available from the
Library of Congress*

ISBN 978-1-009-54373-6 Hardback
ISBN 978-1-009-54371-2 Paperback
ISSN 2977-0327 (online)
ISSN 2977-0319 (print)

Cambridge University Press & Assessment has no responsibility for the
persistence or accuracy of URLs for external or third-party internet websites
referred to in this publication and does not guarantee that any content on
such websites is, or will remain, accurate or appropriate.

For EU product safety concerns, contact us at Calle de José Abascal, 56, 1°, 28003
Madrid, Spain, or email eugpsr@cambridge.org

Origen on Demonic Executioners and the Problem of Evil

Elements in Early Christian Literature

DOI: 10.1017/9781009543750
First published online: January 2026

Ky Heinze
Our Lady Seat of Wisdom College
Author for correspondence: Ky Heinze, kyheinze@seatofwisdom.ca

Abstract: Origen believed that God's providence makes good use of everything, including the actions of wicked demons, which serve to discipline sinners and test the righteous. This Element, which focuses on the disciplinary function of demons, will show that Origen's position was the synthesis and development of a long Jewish and early Christian tradition – a fact not recognized in most scholarship. Disciplinary demons were an important part of Origen's theodicy. According to him, the suffering sinners experience is not the direct action of supposed divine anger, but the wicked attack of demons that is directed (but not caused) by God. Origen's belief that even rebel demons do not escape from fulfilling the divine purpose avoids dualism. This contradicts the frequently expressed view that early Christian intellectuals (particularly Origen) overemphasized Satan's autonomy and endangered the supremacy of God.

Keywords: Origen, demon, evil, providence, executioner

© Ky Heinze 2026

ISBNs: 9781009543736 (HB), 9781009543712 (PB), 9781009543750 (OC)
ISSNs: 2977-0327 (online), 2977-0319 (print)

Contents

1 Origen, Demons, and Theodicy   1
2 Traditions of Punishing Agents   21
3 Punishing Agents in Origen   40

  List of Abbreviations   68

  Bibliography   70

So you see that somehow, for all their cleverness, wicked fairies are dreadfully stupid, for, although from the beginning of the world they have really helped instead of thwarting the good fairies, not one of them is a bit the wiser for it.

George MacDonald, *Little Daylight*

1 Origen, Demons, and Theodicy

This section has two goals: first, to introduce the reader to Origen by identifying his importance and providing a brief outline of his life, work, and thought; and second, to examine Origen's approach to the problem of evil. This examination will focus on how God "uses" evil for good, which is the area in which this Element seeks to contribute.

1.1 Importance of Origen

Origen of Alexandria, who lived from about AD 185 to 254, was a passionate Christian. He was the son of a martyr and the teacher of future martyrs; and he himself died after torture for the faith.[1] He was also the first great Christian scholar.[2] He possessed unparalleled training in textual criticism and philosophical discourse;[3] he founded what might be called the first Christian university[4] and the first major Christian library;[5] and he was one of the most prolific authors in antiquity.[6] Finally, Origen was a public figure who traveled widely, engaged in theological disputes, and was invited to visit and correspond with high administrators and members of the imperial family.[7]

Origen poured both his Christian passion and his professional expertise into the interpretation of the Scriptures, and his vast works with their detailed analyses and "spiritual" interpretations became foundational for Christian exegesis. Origen's belief that Scriptural interpretation is part of an ascetic, prayerful, and mystical journey to God was key to the nascent monastic tradition. Furthermore, he played an important role in defending Christianity before the Roman world, perhaps contributing to the coming Christian ascendency. Origen's life-long polemic against Marcionites and "Gnostics" helped to maintain the Christian link with the Old Testament, the goodness of its God, and the goodness of the

---

[1] Niculescu, "Origen."
[2] Trigg, *Origen* (1983), 8.
[3] Markschies, "Origenes," 1.
[4] McGuckin, *Origen*, 11.
[5] McGuckin, "Caesarea," 20–21; Gamble, *Books and Readers*, 155–61.
[6] Crouzel, *Origen*, 37; Trigg, *Origen* (1983), 245.
[7] Perrone, "Origène," 304.

material world. Integral to all these projects was Origen's effort to build a speculative Christian cosmology that was consistent with the doctrinal standard of the "Rule of Faith" – an effort that both laid the foundation for fourth-century orthodoxy and began certain threads in the tradition that were later condemned.[8]

Origen's reputation, once obscured by controversy, experienced a "renaissance" in the twentieth century.[9] Ongoing manifestations of this are the lively international *Origeniana* conferences and the centers of Origen research in Münster, Germany, and Bologna, Italy. Among Origen's many contributions, scholars have recognized his reflection on Satan and the problem of evil: he is, in Jeffrey Russell's acclaimed words, "the most inventive diabologist of the entire Christian tradition."[10] This Element will contribute to scholarship in this area; but, before identifying this contribution, we begin with a brief outline of Origen's life and work.

1.2 Life of Origen

We know Origen's biography better than that of any other Christian in the first three centuries[11] thanks to Book 6 of Eusebius of Caesarea's *Ecclesiastical History*;[12] but we must read this account with discernment.[13] Origen was born around 185 to Christian parents in Alexandria, Egypt, in the eastern half of the Roman Empire. His father taught him to read and memorize the Scriptures[14] and demonstrated his Christian faith when he suffered martyrdom in 201 under the Egyptian prefect Laetus.[15] This event helped to set the tone for rest of the sixteen-year-old's life.[16] The mother and her many sons had their property confiscated, and they depended on the charity of a wealthy woman until the bright young Origen could

---

[8] On Origen's achievements, see Trigg, *Origen* (1983), 244–46. On his controversial legacy, see Perrone, "Origène," 355–60; Trigg, *Origen* (1983), 246–56.
[9] Perrone, "Origène," 360; Alexandre, "La redécouverte"; Trigg, *Origen* (1983), 256–58.
[10] Russell, *Satan*, 123; Monaci Castagno, *Il diavolo*, 61; Bostock, "Satan," 111.
[11] Perrone, "Origène," 299. For recent accounts of Origen's life, see Perrone, "Origène," 299–309; Markschies, "Origenes," 1–5. McGuckin, "Life of Origen," 1–23; Trigg, *Origen* (1998), 3–61.
[12] In addition, the *Orat. paneg.*, attributed to Gregory Thaumaturgus, gives us the perspective of an admiring student: Trigg, *Origen* (1983), 167–72. On the precious autobiographical moments in Origen's own writings, see Perrone, "Origen's Confessions." Finally, we have the biting attack of Epiphanius of Salamis (*Panarion* 64.1.1–72.9), written over a century after Origen's death.
[13] Nautin, *Origène*.
[14] Eusebius, *Hist. eccl.* 6.2.7–11 (SC 41:84–85); Jerome, *Epist.* 84.8 (CSEL 55:130).
[15] Eusebius, *Hist. eccl.* 6.2.3–6 (SC 41:83–84).
[16] Nautin, *Origène*, 414.

complete his literary training and support his family as a *grammatikos* – a teacher of classical Greek texts.[17]

When catechists became scarce during a new persecution under Aquila (206–10), Origen (now in his early twenties) began teaching Christian doctrine.[18] Eusebius presents Origen as a passionate, compelling teacher who caused a stir by making converts and by publicly standing by them when they were imprisoned and martyred.[19] He eventually forsook his secular teaching career and devoted himself entirely to Christian instruction.[20] Eusebius may be guilty of anachronism when he says that Origen was the third head of a formal Catechetical School in Alexandria;[21] but, his teaching was probably drawn into developing ecclesial institutions under Bishop Demetrius (189–232),[22] and he adhered to the doctrinal standard of the "Rule of Faith."[23]

Origen had the gifts of a quick mind and early intellectual formation; but he also lived in the cultural and intellectual center of the eastern Roman world, and he took full advantage of it. As a *grammatikos*, he became a professional in the Hellenistic tradition of textual criticism and interpretation.[24] Probably through the Christian Clement of Alexandria,[25] he developed a deep familiarity with the work of the first-century Jewish philosopher and exegete Philo of Alexandria;[26] and his conversations with a converted Jew he calls his "Hebrew master" or "teacher"[27] began a lifelong dialogue with Jewish scholars unparalleled among patristic authors until Jerome.[28] Origen also obtained a superb training in Hellenistic philosophy, probably through the instruction of the famous Middle Platonist Ammonius Saccas, who would later teach "the father of Neoplatonism," Plotinus.[29] Finally, Origen's encounter with the schools of Marcion, Valentinus, and Basilides[30] inspired his lifelong mission to

---

[17] Eusebius, *Hist. eccl.* 6.2.11–15 (SC 41:85–86); Trigg, *Origen* (1998), 5.
[18] Eusebius, *Hist. eccl.* 6.3.1–2 (SC 41:86–87).
[19] Eusebius, *Hist. eccl.* 6.3.4–7, 6.4.1–2 (SC 41:87–88, 90–91).
[20] Eusebius, *Hist. eccl.* 6.3.8–9 (SC 41:88–89).
[21] Eusebius, *Hist. eccl.* 6.3.8 (SC 41:88–89).
[22] Perrone, "Origène," 301.
[23] *Princ.* Pref. 2 (Behr, 12); *Comm. Jo.* 32.187–93 (SC 385:268–70); *Comm. ser. Matt.* 33 (GCS 38:59–64); Heine, "Origen," 197–98; Blowers, "Rule of Faith."
[24] Trigg, *Origen* (1998), 5–7.
[25] On Clement and his influence on Origen, see Trigg, *Origen* (1983), 54–66.
[26] Runia, *Philo in Early Christian Literature*; Runia, "Philo of Alexandria."
[27] *Princ.* 1.3.4, 4.3.14 (Behr, 70, 556); *Hom. Jer.* 20.2.2 (SC 238:256).
[28] Dorival and Naiweld, "Les interlocuteurs"; O'Leary, "Judaism"; Sgherri, *Chiesa e Sinagoga*. Niehoff, "Origen's Commentary."
[29] Trigg, *Origen* (1998), 12–14; compare Eusebius, *Hist. eccl.* 6.19 (SC 41:113–19).
[30] Trigg, *Origen* (1983), 38–51.

provide an educated orthodox response.[31] The wealthy Ambrose, one of the spiritually minded Alexandrian intellectuals drawn into these schools, was converted through Origen's teaching and became his patron.[32]

With funds from Ambrose, Origen wrote several initial commentaries and treatises, including *First Principles* (written in 229–30) – a synthetic work of theology that was a landmark in Christian history.[33] As Origen's reputation grew, he began to receive invitations from religious and secular powers outside of Egypt. He visited bishops Alexander of Jerusalem and Theoctistus of Caesarea in Palestine,[34] the Roman governor in Arabia,[35] and the imperial mother, Julia Mamaea, in Antioch.[36] At the same time, personal and doctrinal tensions were developing with Bishop Demetrius of Alexandria. These tensions came to a head in 232, when Bishop Theoctistus of Caesarea ordained Origen a presbyter, while he was on his way to Greece.[37] Demetrius – backed up by an Alexandrian synod and Pontian, Bishop of Rome – condemned the ordination; but, other bishops supported Origen; and he managed to establish himself in Caesarea,[38] where he spent the last two decades of his life.[39]

As a presbyter in Caesarea, Origen regularly preached before the bishop's small congregation[40] and served as a theological expert at local synods.[41] Origen must have had a large correspondence, for Eusebius knew of over 100 letters,[42] and he continued writing commentaries and treatises. Soon after his arrival, Origen's patron, Ambrose, prompted him to write *Prayer* (written in 233–34), which included a compelling defense of prayers of petition against philosophical and Gnostic objections.[43] In addition, Origen became the renowned teacher and master of a personal school that became one of the greatest centers of Christian learning in the third and

---

[31] Perrone, "Origène," 302; compare *Hom. Ps. 77*, 2.4 (GCS 19NS:371–72).
[32] Eusebius, *Hist. eccl.* 6.18.1, 6.23.1–2 (SC 41:112, 123); Perrone, "Origène," 303–4; Monaci Castagno, "Origene e Ambrogio."
[33] Heine, "Origen," 194–99.
[34] Eusebius, *Hist. eccl.* 6.19.15–18 (SC 41:117–19).
[35] Eusebius, *Hist. eccl.* 6.19.15 (SC 41:117).
[36] Eusebius, *Hist. eccl.* 6.21.3 (SC 41:121); Perrone, "Origène," 304.
[37] Eusebius, *Hist. eccl.* 6.23.3–4 (SC 41:123–24).
[38] Eusebius, *Hist. eccl.* 6.26 (SC 41:128–29).
[39] On tensions with Demetrius and the move to Caesarea, see McGuckin, *Origen*, 18–23; Perrone, "Origène," 304–5; Trigg, *Origen* (1983), 130–40.
[40] Monaci Castagno, *Origene predicatore*, 45–64.
[41] McGuckin, *Origen*, 23.
[42] Eusebius, *Hist. eccl.* 6.36.3 (SC 41:139).
[43] Perrone, *La preghiera*, 79–121.

fourth centuries.[44] He employed a Socratic method[45] and used the standard disciplines of dialectic, geometry, astronomy, mathematics, and ethics as a preparation for the higher study of Scripture and theology.[46] For this school Origen begin to collect a library that may have later included 30,000 volumes;[47] it played an important role in the fourth-century Church.[48]

In this period, the Christian relationship with the State continued to be insecure. Only a year or more after Origen's arrival in Caesarea, he wrote *Exhortation to Martyrdom* to Ambrose, who was threatened by the persecution under Maximinus Thrax.[49] Emperor Philip the Arab (reigned 244–49) was favorable to Christianity, and Origen corresponded with him and his wife Severa;[50] but animosity toward Christianity was growing; and Ambrose prompted Origen to write *Against Celsus*, the greatest apologetic work of the third century. It was a Christian response to the Platonist Celsus's old (but apparently influential) anti-Christian treatise.[51] When Philip the Arab was assassinated and the Emperor Decius (reigned 249–51) took power, the first general persecution of Christians took place. Origen suffered a long imprisonment and repeated torture. At the death of Decius, he was released but with a broken body; and he died soon afterward at around age 69, circa 254.[52]

1.3 Exegetical Work of Origen

Origen's explicitly exegetical works vastly outnumber the treatises mentioned earlier, which themselves revolve around the interpretation of Scripture. Based on our sources,[53] we gather that Origen wrote scholarly notes (scholia) on seven books of the Bible[54] and multi-volume commentaries on about thirty-one books. Near the end of his life, Origen finally allowed

---

[44] McGuckin, *Origen*, 11; Rizzi, "La scuola."
[45] Perrone, "Un maître."
[46] *Orat. paneg.* 7.93–15.183 (SC 148:134–72); Origen, *Ep. Greg.* 1 (SC 148:186–88); compare Eusebius, *Hist. eccl.* 6.18.2–4 (SC 41: 112–13); Perrone, "Metodo," 277; Markschies, "Origenes," 5.
[47] Isidore of Seville, *Etymologiae* 6.6 (Lindsay, 226).
[48] McGuckin, "Caesarea," 20–21.
[49] Perrone, "Origène," 329.
[50] Eusebius, *Hist. eccl.* 6.36.3 (SC 41:139).
[51] Perrone, "Origène," 330–32.
[52] Eusebius, *Hist. eccl.* 6.39.5, 7.1 (SC 41:142, 166); Jerome, *De viris illustribus* 54 (Bernoulli, 34); Nautin, *Origène*, 215–18.
[53] Primarily Jerome's *Letter 33 to Paula*, available in English in Crouzel, *Origen*, 37–38.
[54] McGuckin, "Scholarly Works," 26–27.

about 500 of his homilies to be transcribed.[55] This vast corpus of writings makes Origen one of the most prolific authors in antiquity.[56] Partly due to later condemnations of Origen, only a "smoldering ruin"[57] of these works remains, and much of that is not in the original Greek but in the Latin translations of Jerome and Rufinus, the latter having abridged and altered content in keeping with the theological standards of the fourth century.[58] Still, Origen's extant works fill multiple shelves.[59]

Origen's exegetical work shows him to be a master of the skills of a *philologus*.[60] To identify the authentic version of the text, Origen constructed a massive reference work called the *Hexapla*, which contained six parallel columns of different versions of the Old Testament: the Hebrew text, its transliteration into Greek, the Greek Septuagint, and the three later Jewish revisions of the Greek text by Aquila, Symmachus, and Theodotion – Origen added additional texts when he could find them.[61] Origen studied the geography and cities of Palestine, explored the meaning of Hebrew words, consulted scholars in the emerging Rabbinic schools of Caesarea on exegetical matters,[62] and used the major fields of ancient learning to help him understand the text. He was alert to different possible readings (ancient texts lacked punctuation) and to the importance of identifying which character is speaking in a passage; and he analyzed the author's grammar, figures of speech, literary structure, and purpose.[63]

For Origen, inspiration means that the true author of Scripture is the Holy Spirit[64] and that thus its words are "of God" and "not the writings of people."[65] This was the basis for the principal Origen learned from a Jewish convert, that Scripture is the key to interpreting Scripture,[66] which was consonant with the Hellenistic practice of interpreting Homer with

---

[55] Perrone, "Origène," 313.
[56] Crouzel, *Origen*, 37; Trigg, *Origen* (1983), 245.
[57] McGuckin, "Scholarly Works," 25.
[58] Girolami, *L'Oriente*.
[59] For a list of Origen's works and an excellent summary of the state and content of those that remain, see Perrone, "Origène," 309–32; McGuckin, "Scholarly Works," 25–44. On the discovery of 29 of Origen's homilies on the Psalms in the original Greek in 2012, see Perrone, "Origen's New Homilies," 562–74.
[60] Neuschäfer, *Origenes*.
[61] Gentry, "Origen's Hexapla," 553.
[62] de Lange, *Origen*.
[63] Martens, *Origen*, 41–63.
[64] *Princ.* 4.2.7 (Behr, 508); *Comm. Matt.* 14.4 (GCS 40:280–81); *Cels.* 3.3 (SC 136:20).
[65] *Princ.* 4.1.6 (Behr, 474–76). Although, according to Miriam DeCock ("Origen's Sources," 149–59), Origen says relatively little about the Holy Spirit's role in the inspiration of the interpreter.
[66] *Philoc.* 2.1–3 (SC 302:240–44).

Homer.[67] In keeping with this, Origen used his encyclopedic knowledge of Scripture to examine how words and phrases are used throughout its many books, and he collected a "constellation" of related passages[68] to "weave a tapestry" of meaning.[69]

Origen's detailed textual and semantic work went along with an unparalleled emphasis on the spiritual significance of the text. When Jerome praises Origen's *Commentary on the Song of Songs* as the pinnacle of Christian exegesis, he mentions in the same breath his comprehensive analysis of multiple versions of the text (based on the *Hexapla*) and the privileged mystic encounter with God that it helped to achieve: Jerome writes, "It seems to me that in [Origen] the text has been fulfilled: 'The king has brought me into his chamber.'"[70] Jerome's statement shows that Origen took the Shulammite woman in the Song of Songs as a figure of the Church or the soul, searching for God, who is represented by the Shulammite's royal lover.[71] Similarly, Origen often interpreted the Babylonian king Nebuchadnezzar as a figure of the devil, who attacks and takes sinners captive.[72] And he believed the forty-two stages of Israel's journey after their departure from Egypt (Num 33.5–37) represented stages in the soul's journey of salvation.[73]

The idea that important texts have a higher figurative sense was not remarkable in Origen's time. Philosophers read Homer's seedy descriptions of the Olympian gods as allegories for higher truths;[74] and Philo applied a similar method to the Jewish Torah.[75] In Christianity, from the first century on, the Pauline tension between "letter" and "spirit" (2 Cor 3.6) and the conviction that the Old Testament is fulfilled in Christ and the Church involved a certain amount of typological and figurative reading.[76] Under the influence of Philo, Clement of Alexandria developed this element to defend the Old Testament from Marcion and the Gnostics. On the other hand, Gnostics such as Heracleon were using allegory to find Valentinian theology in the gospels.[77] It was in this context that Origen, who claimed

---

[67] Neuschäfer, *Origenes*, 276–85.
[68] Perrone, *La preghiera*, 429–510.
[69] Heine, "Origen," 193.
[70] Jerome, *Orig. Hom. Cant.*, Prologue (SC 37:58), re: Song 1.4.
[71] Chênevert, *L'Église*.
[72] Crouzel, "Diable," 307–8; for example, *Hom. Jer.* 1.3–4 (SC 232:200–2).
[73] *Hom. Num.* 27 (SC 461:270–346); Torjesen, *Hermeneutical Procedure*, 73–77.
[74] Trigg, *Origen* (1983), 32–33.
[75] Niehoff, *Philo*, 173–91.
[76] Crouzel, *Origen*, 64–69.
[77] On the complex relationship between the Gnostics and allegory, see Martens, *Origen*, 114–18.

an apostolic and ecclesial source for his method,[78] became the greatest theorist and practitioner of figurative exegesis in the Christian tradition.[79]

At times, Origen's figurative readings strike one as artificial attempts to make Scripture say what he wishes it said; but many of these readings are based on what he considered the clear teaching of other Scripture passages. We should not underestimate the power and significance of his belief that the Old Testament is not merely a set of Messianic proof texts, but God's message to each soul in its journey to him. We must also recognize that Origen's figurative (or "spiritual") reading was not an ad hoc method but a pattern integral to his entire cosmology and soteriology.[80] It is to this pattern that we now turn, using it as a springboard for a brief outline of Origen's thought.

1.4 Thought of Origen

Origen believed that people at different stages in spiritual development have different needs. As 1 Corinthians 3.1–2 relates, "people of the flesh" are "infants in Christ" who can only drink "milk"; but the more "spiritual" are ready for "solid food." According to Origen, Scripture provides for these different needs by containing three senses or levels of meaning;[81] but in practice he refers to two: the straightforward or literal sense is the "milk" that is beneficial for simple Christians, while the elevated figurative, pneumatic, or anagogical interpretation is the "solid food" needed by those who are more spiritually advanced.[82] Origen believed that the material world is analogous to Scripture[83] in that it contains two aspects:[84] there are external, visible phenomena, which correspond to the literal sense of Scripture; but there is also an inward purpose or meaning or rational pattern (Gk λόγος) that animates or explains these phenomena.[85] Similarly, Christ's visible human flesh indicates his inner divinity. Some see Jesus only "according to the flesh" (cf. 2 Cor 5.16), but those with

---

[78] *Princ.* 4.2.2, 4.2.4 (Behr, 490–500); Perrone, "Metodo," 276–77.
[79] de Lubac, *Exégèse*, 212.
[80] Compare James, *Learning the Language of Scripture.*
[81] *Princ.* 4.2.4 (Behr, 196–98); *Hom. Num.* 9.7 (SC 415:252–56); *Hom. Lev.* 5.1 (SC 286:206); Torjesen, *Hermeneutical Procedure*, 39–43. Origen sees a similar three-step progression in Solomon's trilogy (Proverbs, Ecclesiastes, Song of Songs) and in the transition from law to prophets to gospel: *Hom. Lev.* 1.4.4 (SC 286:80–82).
[82] Origen typically avoids the term "allegorical," due to its association with the philosophical reading of Greek myths. See Simonetti, *Lettera*; Simonetti, *Origene.*
[83] Martens, *Origen*, 195.
[84] Compare *Hom. Gen.* 3.2 (SC 7:116).
[85] *Princ.* 2.11.4, 4.1.7 (Behr, 272–74, 476–78); *Philoc.* 2.4–5 (SC 302:244–48); Perrone, "Looking at the World"; Perrone, "Scrittura," 191.

the right disposition can perceive his divinity, like the disciples at the Transfiguration.[86] On a similar note, Origen believed that Christ's various aspects or titles (ἐπινοίαι) – such as Resurrection, Way, Shepherd, King – correspond to the needs of people at different levels of spiritual development.[87] For example, people who are acting like animals need Christ the Shepherd, but more advanced Christians experience him as King.[88]

The belief that creation, Scripture, and Christ contain a multi-level accommodation to the human condition is fundamental to Origen's thought. It reveals his view that salvation is a journey and that this journey can be expressed by a transition from the outer to the inner, from the literal to the figurative, from the sensible to the invisible, from the fleshly to the spiritual, and from the earthly to the heavenly. This is because the goal of the journey is union with God, who is simple, invisible, limitless,[89] and without passions, save that of charity.[90] In holding this position, which owes something to Middle Platonism and Neopythagoreanism, Origen positioned himself not only against the "simple" Christians he criticized, but also against a considerable number of more educated believers who considered God and the soul to be corporeal or to have a corporeal component.[91] For Origen, one cannot unite with this ineffable God without knowing him; and one cannot know him without loving him beyond earthly things and becoming like him. In other words, the salvific movement from letter to spirit is not a purely intellectual movement but one that requires moral effort, asceticism, and a mystic longing.[92]

It is important to note that, for Origen, human effort is not sufficient for making this spiritual ascent.[93] Occasionally, Origen notes that human free will suffers limitations in its earthly state[94] and that sinners experience a bondage to sin and Satan that requires rescue.[95] The divine

---

[86] *Comm. Matt.* 12.36–37 (GCS 40:150–54); *Hom. Luc.* 20.4 (SC 87:282–84); *Cels.* 2.64 (SC 132:434–36); Harl, *Origène*; Pettits, "Transfiguration."
[87] Perrone, "Scrittura," 177–78n15.
[88] Trigg, *Origen* (1983), 97–98.
[89] *Princ.* 1.1.6 (Behr, 30–34); *Comm. Jo.* 1.20.119 (SC 120:120); Perrone, "Origène," 338; Trigg, *Origen* (1983), 95.
[90] *Hom. Ezech.* 6.6.3 (SC 352:228–30); *Hom. Ps. 77*, 9.1 (GCS 19NS:467); *Comm. Matt.* 13.2 (GCS 40:183); Perrone, "Origène," 340–41; Fernández, "Passio."
[91] For example, Melito of Sardis (second century), some present at Origen's *Dialogue with Heraclides*, and the "anthropomorphite" monks who were still influential in Alexandria in the fourth century: Perrone, "Origène," 330, 337, 356.
[92] Crouzel, *Origène et la Connaissance*, for example, 409; Martens, *Origen*, 162–67, esp. n3.
[93] de Lubac, *Histoire*; O'Leary, "Grace"; *Hom. Jer.* 6.2.5 (SC 232:334).
[94] Perrone, "Libero arbitrio."
[95] Compare Alcain, *Cautiverio*, 145–61, 305–12.

accommodation in Scripture and the incarnation (mentioned earlier) is critical. In addition, Origen says that Christ's death broke Satanic power, ransomed sinners from his control, and made forgiveness through baptism possible. Martyrs, too, bring relief to those oppressed by demons.[96]

As a final note, Origen's concept that the multiple aspects of natural phenomena, Scripture, and Christ are accommodations to the needs of individuals also expresses itself in his view of providence.[97] As Hal Koch observed, Origen generally considered providence (πρόνοια) to be a process of education (παίδευσις).[98] God tailor makes for each person the birth, circumstances, and life experiences that are ideal for inducing that person's conversion. This includes God's orchestration of the work of bishops, presbyters, and guardian angels, who are God's ministers to promote the salvation of their charges:[99] Origen's soteriology is cooperative and communal. To describe God's providential work, Origen uses several metaphors: God is the loving Father who arranges household affairs (as an οἰκόνομος) for his children;[100] he (or, more properly, Christ) is the physician who heals their souls[101] and the teacher (or παιδαγωγός) who trains them for salvation.[102]

We have now seen that God's works include creation, providence, Scripture, and the incarnation of the Son; and Origen argues that, because God is good, the purpose of all his works must be to save rational creatures.[103] This is accomplished by communicating the saving knowledge of God and by imposing a program of moral, ascetic, and mystical training and healing. This communication and training is a multi-stage affair, corresponding to the different stages in spiritual growth; and this explains why all of God's works have, in addition to their outer or superficial level, a deeper level that reveals itself to those who are ready for it.

This concludes our brief outline of Origen's importance, life, work, and thought, setting the stage for the second half of this section, which will examine his approach to the problem of evil.

---

[96] *Comm. Jo.* 6.281–87 (SC 157:342–48); *Comm. Rom.* 2.9.34 (SC 532:410); *Comm. Matt.* 16.8 (GCS 40:498–99).
[97] *Hom. Jer.* 6.2.5 (SC 232:334).
[98] Koch, *Pronoia*, 30–31.
[99] *Hom. Ps. 37* 1.1 (SC 411:258–72); *Princ.* 1.6.2, 2.1.2, 2.9.8, 3.5.4–6 (Behr, 108, 146, 250, 432–34); Bettencourt, *Doctrina*, 27–28.
[100] Widdicombe, *Fatherhood*; Nemeshegyi, *La paternité*.
[101] Fernández, *Cristo*, 64.
[102] Koch, *Pronoia*.
[103] Compare *Hom. Gen.* 3.2 (SC 7:116–18).

1.5 The Problem of Evil in Origen

How can God be good if there is evil in the world? One solution to this "problem of evil" is to limit God's sphere of responsibility.[104] Marcionites and Gnostics reduced the high God's responsibility by saying he was not the creator of this flawed world or the God of the Old Testament,[105] but of course Origen disagreed.[106] Epicureans denied providence[107] and Aristotelians limited divine responsibility for the administration of this messy world by saying that it did not extend below the region of the moon;[108] but again, as we have just seen above, Origen disagreed. Making use of some Middle Platonic arguments,[109] he advocated a daring Christian[110] vision in which divine providence concerns itself with the lives (and even the prayers) of individuals, omitting not even the falling of a sparrow (re: Matt 10.29–30).[111] According to Origen, God's providence includes foreseeing human actions and incorporating them into his plan; but he does not cause them.[112] Thus, for Origen, free will is the one thing for which God is not responsible; and this is at the center of his theodicy.

The problem of evil can be eased, not just by limiting God's sphere of responsibility, but also by a stern definition of divine "goodness." For the Jewish-leaning Christian apologist Theophilus of Antioch (second century),[113] the providentially "good, beneficent, and merciful" God is also a "fire" in "his wrath" (ὀργὴν) and the "judge and punisher (κολαστὴς) of the ungodly."[114] Origen's Western contemporary Tertullian was quite comfortable with a God who deals out death, vengeance, and eternal damnation;[115] and he rhapsodizes about the exultation (*exultare*) of watching proud sinners and persecutors burn in hell.[116] Obviously, Theophilus and Tertullian felt little dissonance with Scripture passages

---

[104] Compare Cels. 4.3 (SC 136:192–94).
[105] *Philoc.* 23.2 (SC 226:136–40).
[106] Trigg, *Origen* (1983), 39–47, 50, 71–72.
[107] *Comm. Rom.* 3.1.13 (SC 539:52).
[108] *Cels.* 1.21 (SC 132:128); *Comm. Rom.* 3.1.14 (SC 539:52–54); Perrone, "Provvidenza," 392.
[109] Perrone, "Provvidenza," 395–96; Junod, "Introduction," 85.
[110] Benjamins, *Eingeordnete Freiheit*, 166–211.
[111] *Comm. Rom.* 3.1.13 (SC 539:52); *Hom. Luc.* 32.3 (SC 87:388); *Hom. Gen.* 3.2 (SC 7:114–16); *Princ.* 1.2.9 (Behr, 54); Cels. 1.9 (SC 132:100); Cels. 4.14 (SC 136:216–18); Burns, *Did God Care?*, 128–31.
[112] *Philoc.* 23.8 (SC 226:154–58); *Or.* 6.3–5 (GCS 3:313–15); Benjamins, *Eingeordnete Freiheit*, Chap. 3.
[113] Rogers, "Theophilus," 214, 16, 18, 23.
[114] *Autol.* 1.3 (Grant, 4).
[115] *Pud.* 13.15–22 (CCSL 2:1305–6); *Marc.* 5.16.1–6 (Evans, 608–12).
[116] *Spect.* 30.2–7 (SC 332:318–28); Trigg, *Origen* (1983), 114–15, 224.

about divine judgment. On a similar note, Origen says that "simple" Christians are not offended by the literal interpretation of disturbing stories about God in Scripture and thus "suppose things about him that would not even be supposed about the most savage and unjust person."[117] In contrast, Origen believed that the transcendent and incorporeal God is never offended or angry, that his "punishments" are beneficial, and that he does not condemn people to eternal suffering.[118] He supported his position with Scripture passages about divine love; but he was also indebted to a Platonic and religious current of thought that flowed in figures such as Philo, Plutarch, Clement of Alexandria, and, ironically, the heterodox schools of Marcion, Valentinus, and Basilides.[119] This meant that Origen felt the discomfort with passages about supposed divine vindictiveness, cruelty, and limitation that had caused Marcion and some Gnostics to reject the Old Testament, even if he did not do so.[120]

Thus, Origen did not repudiate the Old Testament or the Creator. He also had a strong sense of divine providence and an exalted vision of divine goodness and transcendence. In this expansive and audacious vision, all the messiness and ugliness in this world and in Scripture had to be reconciled with the supreme goodness of God. Understandably, Origen's answers to the problem of evil, to which we now turn, were expansive and integral to the structure of his thought.

1.5.1 Free Will

As just noted, the core of Origen's theodicy is that rational creatures possess free will and that God is not responsible for its misuse.[121] In Origen's time, the freedom of the will was not to be taken for granted. There was a cultural conviction that humans are caught in the grip of fate, which is determined by the stars or by the necessary, causal succession of events posited by some Stoics.[122] With regard to Scripture, Origen had to address the possibility that Judas was destined to sin by the prophecies that predicted his betrayal of Jesus.[123] Paul's discussion of God's "authority" to make some people vessels "for honor" and others "vessels of wrath prepared

---

[117] *Princ.* 4.2.1 (Behr, 488).
[118] For example, *Cels.* 4.72 (SC 136:360–64); *Hom. Ps. 77* 6.1 (GCS 19NS:423–25); Trigg, *Origen* (1983), 114–15, 86, 224; Crouzel, *Origen*, 243–44, 57–66.
[119] Trigg, *Origen* (1983), 41, 45–47, 49, 50, 73–74; Stroumsa, "Incorporeality," 348.
[120] *Princ.* 4.2.1 (Behr, 484–88).
[121] *Princ.* 2.9.6 (Behr, 246).
[122] *Philoc.* 23.1 (SC 226:130–36); *Princ.* 3.5.5 (Behr, 432); Trigg, *Origen* (1983), 37.
[123] *Cels.* 2.20 (SC 132:336–44); Laeuchli, "Origen's Interpretation," 261.

for destruction" (re: Rom 9.21–22) might mean that he determines their moral disposition.[124] On that note, Satan and his demons might be examples of creatures damned by nature.[125] According to Origen, Valentinian Gnostics pointed to these things to prove their belief that people have different natures with different potentials for salvation.[126] Finally, some Christians thought that demonic impulses to sin rendered the human will helpless.[127]

For Origen, the determinism posited by astrology or Stoicism or Valentinianism would make God responsible for sin.[128] In that case, the countless moral exhortations in Scripture would be useless, and the Christian doctrine of God's judgment of sinners, including rewards for the righteous and condemnation for the wicked, would be hideously unjust.[129] In addition to these observations, Origen confronted specific arguments against free will. He claimed that Biblical prophecy and astrological predictions (to the extent that they exist and can be read by angels) do not cause the future.[130] Prophecy is based on God's foreknowledge of the actions that humans will freely make. Thus, Judas' sin was the cause of the prophecies about him, and not the other way around.[131] Similarly, Origen argued that the Pauline idea of predestination does not mean that God determines people's moral disposition but simply that he foresees what it will be.[132]

Against the Valentinians, Origen argued that Satan was evil by choice, not by nature.[133] Origen followed second-century Christian authors in identifying Satan as one of the fallen angels mentioned in post-exilic Judaism and the New Testament.[134] Many Christians, guided by the Book of the Watchers, held that these angels were the "sons of God" in Genesis 6.2 who had fallen due to their lust for women and had spawned

---

[124] *Comm. Rom.* 7.14–15 (SC 543:380–402). For Origen's discussion of multiple passages thought to negate free will, see *Princ.* 3.1.7–24 (Behr, 300–78).
[125] *Comm. Jo.* 20.198–219 (SC 290:254–64); Crouzel, "Le démoniaque," 10.
[126] *Comm. Matt.* 10.11 (SC 162:176–84). But many scholars now doubt that Valentinianism was deterministic: for example, Norelli, "Marcione."
[127] *Princ.* 3.2.1 (Behr, 382); Monaci Castagno, "La demonologia origeniana," 236.
[128] *Princ.* 3.5.5 (Behr, 432); *Comm. Jo.* 20.202 (SC 290:254); Crouzel, "Le démoniaque," 10.
[129] *Princ.* 3.1.6 (Behr, 296–300).
[130] *Philoc.* 23.15–16 (SC 226:178–86); Koch, *Pronoia*, 114–15; Hall, "Origen," 117–19.
[131] *Philoc.* 23.8–9 (SC 226:154–60). This is an "innovation" of Origen, according to Burns, *Did God Care?*, 313–14.
[132] Scheck, *Origen*, 25–29.
[133] *Princ.* 1.5.2–3 (Behr, 90–96); Monaci Castagno, "Diavolo," 114. But Origen thought that Satan's evil habits might become "some sort of nature": *Princ.* 1.6.3 (Behr, 114 and 115n68).
[134] *Princ.* Pref. 2, 6 (Behr, 12, 16); Monaci Castagno, *Il diavolo*, 63.

violent giants whose enduring spirits were the demons of the earth.[135] Disturbingly, some Gnostics pointed out that such demons would be evil by nature.[136] Another problem was that Satan must have been evil long before the events of Genesis 6, since Christians associated him with the tempting serpent of Eden (Gen 3.1): how, then, could he be the chief of the demons? Monaci Castagno shows how Origen untangled this "intricate knot."[137] According to him, the fall of Satan and his angels was not lust for women before the flood or envy of Adam and Eve in Eden,[138] but rather pride or boredom with God before the creation of the material world, perhaps in the "preexistence" (see Section 1.5.3).[139] Origen found references to Satan's fall, not in Genesis 6.2,[140] but in a rich array of other verses interpreted figuratively.[141] Aspects of Origen's solution became the standard in Christian thought.

1.5.2 Puzzling and Painful Divine Acts

Through the arguments above, Origen defended free will and argued that it, not God, is responsible for moral evil; but he still had to show that the all-encompassing providence he envisioned is benevolent, even when life seems cruel and unfair.[142] Given the analogy he envisioned between the various works of God,[143] Origen believed that this problem is similar, whether one encounters troubling things in created phenomenon, life experiences, or the pages of Scripture.[144] In every case, one must pray for divine help and practice humility and faith. One must not reject the works of God (like the heretics), and one must trust that there will eventually be explanations.[145]

---

[135] 1 Enoch 6–7, 9.7–11, 15–16 (trans. by Nickelsburg and VanderKam, 23–25, 27, 36–38). On the Watchers' account, see: Stokes, *The Satan*, 60–73. For its influence on early Christianity, see the scholarship cited in Burns, *Did God Care?*, 136–37n52.

[136] Janssens, "La thème," 490–94; Filoramo, *L'attesa*, 150–55.

[137] Monaci Castagno, "La demonologia origeniana," 234–35.

[138] Bostock, "Satan," 112; Russell, *Satan*, 79n10, 93, 105; Kelly, *Satan*, 138–41.

[139] Thompson, "Demonology"; Roukema, "Origen," 207; Monaci Castagno, *Il diavolo*, 102n252, 103; Monaci Castagno, "La demonologia origeniana," 235–36; Crouzel, "Le démoniaque," 6–9, 11; Russell, *Satan*, 126.

[140] *Cels*. 5.52–55 (SC 147:146–54), but note the exception in *Hom. Jes. Nav*. 15.3 (SC 71:336). See Monaci Castagno, *Il diavolo*, 63n145; Bostock, "Satan," 112; Tzvetkova-Glaser, "Evil," 184; compare Burns, *Did God Care?*, 131n35.

[141] Ezek 28.1–19; Isa 14:12–22; Job 40:19 (LXX); *Princ*. 1.5.4–5 (Behr, 96–104); Monaci Castagno, *Il diavolo*, 102n252; Monaci Castagno, *Origene predicatore*, 158–59.

[142] Burns, *Did God Care?*, 131–32.

[143] *Hom. Gen*. 3.2 (SC 7:114–16); *Philoc*. 2.4–5 (SC 302:244–48).

[144] *Princ*. 4.1.7 (Behr, 476–78); *Princ*. 2.11.4–7 (Behr, 272–80); *Philoc*. 2.4–5 (SC 302:244–48); *Hom. Ps. 76* (LXX) 3.4 (GCS 19NS:338); Perrone, "Scrittura," 191.

[145] *Princ*. 4.1.7 (Behr, 476–78); *Philoc*. 1.28 (SC 302:200–2); Martens, *Origen*, 168, 78–91.

Origen worked hard to find such explanations. He did not know why snakes exist,[146] but he suggested that the difficulty of human survival on the earth, which initially seems inconsistent with the benevolence of providence, forces humans to use their intellects and preserve their likeness to God.[147] With regard to Scripture, Origen argued that references to God doing "evil" (e.g. Mic 1.12) refer to his providential use (κατὰ πρόνοιαν) of suffering to discipline sinners (ὑπὲρ τοῦ παιδευθῆναι).[148] He also believed that providence uses suffering to test and glorify the righteous and to bring spiritual relief to others. Thus, according to Origen, suffering is not a true "evil,"[149] any more than the harsh (but healing) remedies of a doctor are evil.[150] Similarly, Origen believed that, whenever God "kills," he does so only to "make alive" (re: Deut 32.39).[151] He thought there were indications that the deaths of Pharaoh,[152] Ananias, and Sapphira (re: Acts 5.1–11) were salvific.[153] Although Origen generally accepted the validity of both literal and figurative reading, he believed that accounts with impossible or inappropriate content had no historic basis and were only intended to indicate higher meanings.[154] God's command to slaughter the Canaanites, which Origen takes figuratively as a command to annihilate sin, may be an example of this, since Origen deplores the idea that "holy" people would literally engage in such acts.[155]

1.5.3 Preexistence of Souls

Pain or injustice suffered from the moment of birth was particularly difficult to interpret as just discipline for sin or salutary pedagogy. In *First Principles* 2.9.5, Origen asks why some humans were born among savage cannibals and others among the divinely guided Hebrews. Why

---

[146] *Philoc.* 2.5 (SC 302: 246–48).
[147] *Cels.* 4.74, 4.76 (SC 136:366–76).
[148] *Philoc.* 26.8 (SC 226:264).
[149] *Philoc.* 26.3 (SC 226:242–46).
[150] *Hom. Exod.* 8.5 (SC 321:264–66); *Hom. Jer.* 6.2.1–4 (SC 232:330–34); *Hom. Ezech.* 1.1–2 (SC 352:36–38). This is consistent with principles in Plutarch, Clement of Alexandria, and Gnostics such as Heracleon and Basilides (Trigg, *Origen* (1983), 41, 45–46, 56; Daniélou, *Origène*, 98.); but it also derives from the core Christian belief in the God who suffers and redeems (*Hom. Ezech.* 6: SC 352:212–46); Perrone, "Provvidenza," 393.
[151] *Cels.* 2.24 (SC 132:350); *Hom. Luc.* 16.4–7 (SC 87:240–46); *Comm. Matt.* 15.11 (GCS 40:377–80); *Hom. Ps.* 77, 7.7 (GCS 19NS:447); *Hom. Jer.* 1.16 (SC 232:232–36), re: Jer 1.9–10.
[152] Harl, "La mort."
[153] *Philoc.* 27.8 (SC 226: 294).
[154] *Princ.* 4.2.3–4.3.3 (Behr, 492–526); Crouzel, *Origen*, 62–64.
[155] *Hom. Jes. Nav.* 8.7 (SC 71:234, 238); Trigg, *Origen* (1983), 186.

was Jacob loved before birth and Esau hated?[156] For that matter, why are some rational creatures glorious angels in heaven and others lowly humans on the earth? Why are there different ranks of angels?[157] According to Origen, the good and just God must have originally created all rational creatures "equal and identical."[158] They were glorious "intellects" (νόες), clothed in aethereal bodies, contemplating God in perfection. According to a hypothesis expressed primarily in *First Principles*,[159] these intellects sinned through varying degrees of neglect or boredom with the good.[160] As a result, God created the material world and gave each the body type, rank, and experiences that corresponded to its sin and were needed for its training. Those with minimal or no sin were clothed in astral or angelic bodies to minister to lower creatures; those who sinned moderately were incarnate in the heavy bodies of humans; and those who sinned most became demons. Thus, even one's cosmic rank and the circumstances of one's birth can be seen as providential justice and discipline for sin.

Although we must remember that Origen rejected reincarnation, his hypothesis may be conceptually related to the Platonic belief that sins in prior earthly lives explain present suffering,[161] an idea that merged with Jewish thinking in Philo and appears in some Gnostic texts.[162] While some scholars believe the theory of the preexistence to be structural to Origen's thought,[163] others are doubtful and point to Origen's possible belief that future sins, as well as preexistent sins, explain present suffering.[164] Outside of *First Principles*, Origen's references to the preexistence are less explicit, and he observes that what happened before the historical economy of salvation is veiled to us.[165] At the same time, his repeated claim that Satan was the first to sin and become incarnate[166] seems to present Satan's

---

[156] Re: Mal 1.2–3; Rom 9.10–13.
[157] *Princ.* 2.9.5 (Behr, 242–44).
[158] *Princ.* 2.9.6 (Behr, 244–46).
[159] *Princ.* 1.6.2–3, 2.6.3, 2.8.3, 2.9.4–8, 3.1.23, 3.5.4–5 (Behr, 106–14, 206–8, 226–32, 242–50, 370–74, 428–32).
[160] Roukema, "Origen," 206–8; Harl, "Recherches."
[161] Bostock, "Sources"; Trigg, *Origen* (1983), 68–69.
[162] Yli-Karjanmaa, *Reincarnation*; Givens, *When Souls Had Wings*, 39–70; Trigg, *Origen* (1983), 41.
[163] Daniélou, *Origène*, 207–17; Simonetti, "Due note"; Crouzel, *Origen*, 205–18; Trigg, *Origen* (1983), 103–7; Gasparro, "Eguaglianza." See also Gasparro's articles on "Caduta," "Creazione," and "Preesistenza" in Monaci Castagno, *Origene: dizionario*.
[164] Edwards, *Origen*, 88–96; Edwards, *Problem of Evil*, 152–56. The passages typically cited in support are *Or.* 6.4–5 (GCS 3:313–15); *Princ.* 3.1.2 (Behr, 286); *Comm. Rom.* 7.13–14 (SC 543:374–92).
[165] *Hom. Ps. 76*, 4.5 (GCS 19NS:349); *Hom. Isa.* 1.2, 4.1 (GCS 33:245, 257–58); Perrone, "Origène," 339.
[166] *Comm. Jo.* 1.97–98 (SC 120:106–8); *Comm. Jo.* 20.176–82 (SC 290:244–48); *Cels.* 6.44 (SC 147:288).

fall as the descent of one of the preexistent intellects to a demonic state.[167] Some, however, think that Origen describes two Satanic falls: one in which his intellect descended to the rank of angel (possibly due to sin) and the other in which he fell from his angelic state.[168]

1.5.4 The Use of Evil for Good

As we discussed earlier, Origen believed that divine providence uses suffering to discipline and train. But suffering is often caused by evil people or, at least in the ancient view, evil demons, who create plagues, droughts, and civil discord.[169] This implies that providence uses human and demonic wickedness, which, in fact, is an important element in Origen's theodicy.

According to Origen, God allows evil in this world because darkness reveals the splendor of light and bitterness the sweetness of honey. He means that the vices of the wicked reveal the splendor of the virtuous but also that the attacks of the wicked challenge the righteous to prove themselves and gain glory. Origen mentions the attacks of wicked humans, but his main emphasis is on those of demons.[170] God calls the sea monsters of Genesis 1.21–22, which represent demons, "good" because they provide a "contest" in which the righteous, like Job, can win "double glory."[171] "If you remove the devil himself and the opposing powers that struggle against us, the virtues of the soul will not shine forth,"[172] and "none of Christ's athletes" will be able to compete for victory and reward.[173] In these passages, Origen is careful to say that God does not cause evil but merely that he "uses it" (*utitur ea*) for "good" and "necessary causes." Creatures become "vessel<s> of reproach"[174] through their own choice. But then, "through the justice and ineffable reason of his providence," God "dispenses" (*dispensat*) or "makes use of evil vessels for his good work" (*uasis malis utitur Deus ad opus bonum*).[175]

---

[167] Heine, *Origen: Commentary*, 53n149; Crouzel, "Le démoniaque," 9.
[168] Monaci Castagno, "La demonologia origeniana," 235–36; Thompson, "Demonology"; Russell, *Satan*, 126. Compare Simonetti, "Due note."
[169] *Cels.* 8.31 (SC 150:242); Monaci Castagno, "La demonologia cristiana," 237–38; Russell, *Satan*, 133; Bettencourt, *Doctrina*, 47–51.
[170] *Hom. Num.* 9.1.5 (SC 415:228–30).
[171] *Hom. Gen.* 1.10 (SC 7:48–50).
[172] *Hom. Num.* 9.1.5 (SC 415:228–30).
[173] *Hom. Num.* 13.7.2, 14.2.5 (SC 442:146–48, 168–70).
[174] Re: 2 Tim 2.20–21; Rom 9.21–23.
[175] *Hom. Num.* 14.2.1, 14.2.6 (SC 442:164–66, 170); *Princ.* 2.1.2 (Behr, 146); compare *Or.* 29.17–30.3 (GCS 3:391–95); *Hom. Luc.* 26.4 (SC 87:340–42).

According to Origen, demons are not only useful in challenging the righteous: they also "provide a service for the divine will"[176] by punishing sinners. In fact, an evil spirit is sometimes "sent out from the Lord ... like an executioner" (*tamquam carnifex*). God "uses" (*abutitur*) such a spirit, but it chooses to deceive by its "own intention and will" (re: 1 Kgs 22.22).[177] In *Against Celsus*, Origen says perhaps these "executioners" (δήμιοι) have "received authority" through some kind of "divine decision" (κρίσει τινὶ θείᾳ) and "have been assigned (τεταγμένοι) to certain [tasks] by the Logos of God who administers the whole world." Nevertheless, these "wretched demons," not God, are the direct perpetrators (αὐτουργοῦσι) of the violence they commit.[178] For Origen, "all creatures and spirits ... serve God and provide to him the service for which they have shown themselves suited." For those "of depraved and evil intent,"[179] this means being a messenger of God's wrath[180] or exacting "taxes of the flesh" from sinners through "various trials."[181]

Origen also expresses this by saying that God "hands over" fallen Christians to Satan for discipline.[182] Perhaps we can compare this to Origen's idea that God sometimes abandons people to suffer extended bondage to sin, as when he "hardened" Pharaoh's heart.[183] God does this because immediate discipline and a quick cure does not permanently heal people like Pharaoh, in whom the sickness of sin has become deep (εἰς βάθος). They need to wallow in wickedness for an extended period in order to turn away from it definitively.[184] As Origen explains, the sin to which God "gives over" people (re: Rom 1.23–27) is its own punishment, but this is a cleansing and remedial punishment.[185] On a similar note, Origen says it is "more advantageous" to be "in wickedness" than to be

---

[176] *divinae voluntati exhibent ministerium.*
[177] *propositum suum voluntatemque.* Comm. Rom. 7.1.3 (SC 543:246–48); Princ. 3.2.1 (Behr, 380–82).
[178] Cels. 7.70, 8.31–32 (SC 150:176, 240–44).
[179] Comm. Rom. 9.30.1–2 (SC 555:178).
[180] Compare 1 Cor 5.5, 1 Tim 1.20; Hom. Ps. 77, 7.7 (GCS 19NS:446); Comm. Rom. 1.19.3 (SC 532:238–40); Schol. Apoc. 30 (Tzamalikos, 159–61); Cels. 4.71–73 (SC 163:358–66); Hom. Num. 9.5.1–3 (SC 415:242–44).
[181] Comm. Rom. 9.30.3 (SC 555:180–82); Hom. Luc. 35.3–15 (SC 87:414–28); Hom. Luc. 23.5–9 (SC 87:316–22).
[182] Hom. Ezech. 12.3–4 (SC 352:388–92); Hom. Jer. 1.3–4 (SC 232:200–2); Fr. Jer. 48.125 (GCS 6:222); Hom. Jes. Nav. 7.6–7 (SC 71:208–14); Comm. Matt. 16.8, 17.14 (GCS 40:496, 625); Philoc. 27.8 (SC 226:296).
[183] Re: Exod 4.21; Rom 9.18.
[184] Princ. 3.1.13, 17 = Philoc. 21.12, 16 (Behr, 326–28, 342–44); Or. 29.13–15 (GCS 3:387–91); Trevijano Etcheverria, *En lucha*, 318.
[185] Or. 29.15 (GCS 3:389–91).

"lukewarm" (re: Rev 3.15), for those who wholly "cling to the flesh" will become so nauseated with its vices that they may "be converted more easily and quickly from material baseness to spiritual grace and the desire for heavenly things."[186] Thus, in God's remarkable providence, sin itself plays a role in achieving salvation.

The divine use of evil, outlined earlier in its various forms, is the topic of this Element; but there will only be space for a detailed analysis of one aspect of the idea: the role of punishing demons or divine "executioners." Here, however, we will make some comments on the topic in general in the context of existing scholarship. This scholarship regularly notes Origen's belief that God uses evil demons for good,[187] sometimes calling it "radical,"[188] but it rarely examines the network of Scriptural passages on which he depends.[189] These passages reveal that Origen has synthesized and updated a many-faceted post-exilic Jewish and early Christian tradition, which is the focus of Section 2. The only scholar who has identified this is Dylan Burns in his helpful work *Did God Care?* (2020). As we shall see, scholars have long studied the relevant theme in Scripture, and recent contributions feature God's use of evil and the devil's role as "God's executioner" or "minister of justice."[190] These scholars, however, make no reference to the corresponding theme in Origen, even when he features in their studies.[191] The interaction between Origen's punishing demons and the mediating beings of Platonism has been better explored,[192] but references to God's human and demonic "executioners" in Philo and Plutarch still need to be taken into account.

In addition to this lack of contextualization, only a few scholars have examined the functions played by the divine use of evil in Origen's thought. Hal Koch (1932) reasons that free will was not sufficient for Origen's theodicy, because it explains only the beginning, not the continuation, of

---

[186] *Princ.* 3.4.3 (Behr, 418).
[187] Burns, *Did God Care?*, 132–35, 51; Bostock, "Satan," 118–19; Tzvetkova-Glaser, "Evil," 188; Monaci Castagno, "Diavolo," 116; Crouzel, "Le démoniaque," 32, 39; Crouzel, "Celse," 34, 40; Russell, *Satan*, 133–34; Recheis, *Engel*, 79–84; Rahner, "La doctrine," 87–88, 422, 37, 43; Daniélou, *Origène*, 238–39; Koch, *Pronoia*, 118–31; Edwards, *Problem of Evil*, 159.
[188] Burns, *Did God Care?*, 135; Bostock, "Satan," 118.
[189] Exceptions are Recheis, *Engel*, 77–84; Rahner, "La doctrine," 434–37, who examines Origen's reception of 1 Cor 5.5; Burns, *Did God Care?*, who identifies the tradition from which Origen draws but does not examine his reception of it in detail.
[190] Stokes, *The Satan*; Kelly, *Satan*; Thornton, "Satan as Adversary"; Thornton, "Satan: God's Agent"; Hamori, "Spirit"; Page, "Satan."
[191] Kelly, *Satan*, 142–45.
[192] Burns, *Did God Care?*, 132–35, 51.

evil. To explain why God allows evil to continue, argues Koch, Origen observed that God can use it for good.[193] Gerald Bostock (2011) appears to agree, calling God's use of evil "an indisputable aspect of Origen's theodicy."[194] This is especially evident in Origen's *Homilies on Numbers*, where he explains why God has not yet "removed the devil from his sovereignty over this age."[195] God could prohibit (*prohibet*) evil, but he does not, because he "makes use of it for necessary reasons."[196] Similarly, a city does not eliminate even "the worst of people, who live a vile and secret life," because it finds they "provide a benefit" by performing tasks such as cleaning latrines.[197] Without the wickedness of Joseph's brothers and the betrayal of Judas Iscariot, God's plan of earthly and eternal salvation would not have been accomplished.[198] Thus, God's providence allows things to remain that people feel "should be repudiated and cast off," because these things "end up having some kind of a necessary function." In God's plan, "nothing is useless or superfluous."[199]

The idea Koch identifies – that God's use of evil explains why he lets sin continue – appears primarily in Origen's discussions of demons who test the righteous, while this Element focuses on demons who punish sinners. There are, however, two other functions of God's use of evil in Origen's thought that pertain to both testing and punishing. Section 3 will discuss these functions in detail, so only a brief outline appears here. Koch showed how God's use of evil functions to defend God's goodness; but, it can also function to defend God's supremacy. According to the Platonist Celsus, one point against Christianity was that God would not be God if his will could be challenged by a superhuman rebel such as Satan.[200] Christians, too, seem to have worried that demon-inspired persecutions showed that God was not in control. Part of Origen's response, as Kurt Flasch (2019) correctly observes,[201] is that Satan and the persecuting powers, far from challenging God's supremacy, are merely pawns in the hands of divine providence.

Origen also employs God's use of evil to make the point that God himself does not do evil but merely providentially arranges the evil done

---

[193] Koch, *Pronoia*, 119–24.
[194] Bostock, "Satan," 118–19.
[195] *Hom. Num.* 13.7.2 (SC 442:148).
[196] *Hom. Num.* 14.2.1 (SC 442:166).
[197] *Hom. Num.* 14.2.6–7 (SC 442:170–72); *Hom. Gen.* 1.10 (SC 7:48–50).
[198] *Hom. Num.* 14.2.4 (SC 442:168).
[199] *Hom. Num.* 9.1.1 (SC 415:222).
[200] *Cels.* 6.42 (SC 147:278–84).
[201] Flasch, *Le Diable*, 77–79.

by his creatures. Thus, the idea functions both to show God's power over evil and to distance him from it. Burns, I think, recognizes this twin functionality when he says that some early Christian intellectuals, including Origen, inherited the "attenuated dualism" of Judaism.[202] With regard to distancing God from evil, Origen believes that sinners rightly suffer wrath, pain, bondage, and indebtedness; but he tends to say that God is not the torturer or slaver or creditor – Satan and his demons, working as God's ministers, are often said to fill these roles. Although this kind of theodicy has not received sufficient analysis in Origen, it has been well studied (and perhaps overplayed) in scholarship on satan figures in early Jewish and first-century Christian writings.[203]

2 Traditions of Punishing Agents

The purpose of this section is to identify the Jewish and early Christian sources of Origen's (and other patristic writers') belief that God uses Satan and his demons to test the righteous and punish sinners, with a focus on the second role. We will also briefly consider the possible confluence of this idea with parallel concepts in Greek religion and Hellenistic philosophy. One conclusion of this section will be that the idea of God's use of evil can serve both to assert God's supremacy over evil and to distance God from evil. To begin with, however, we will consider why scholars who address God's use of evil (either in Biblical studies or Historical Theology) tend to overlook the patristic reception of the idea.

2.1 The "Rise" of Satan

A grand narrative of Satan's "history,"[204] which I find somewhat problematic, guides much of the scholarship on God's use of evil. According to this narrative, YHWH in the Hebrew Bible is (or appears to be) the source of evil as well as of good (cf. Isa 45.7).[205] Post exilic Jews struggled to reconcile this with their growing sense that God is purely good. The solution, which is thought by some to show the influence of Iranian dualism, was to take the spirits and angelic agents that God used for his

---

[202] Burns, *Did God Care?*, 135–36, 49.
[203] Forsyth, *Old Enemy*; Theißen, "Monotheismus." For an argument that such claims are overplayed, see Wasserman, *Apocalypse*.
[204] For recent contributions, see Wright, *Satan*; Flasch, *Le Diable*; Hamori, "Early History"; Stokes, *The Satan*.
[205] Theißen, "Monotheismus," 50; Stokes, *The Satan*, 1; Wright, *Satan*, 2; Flasch, *Le Diable*, 25; Hamori, "Early History," 86; Russell, *Satan*, 219.

harsher actions and begin blaming them for the evil that God seemed to do.[206] For some, the highly disputed passages on the story of David's census illustrate the principle. In 2 Samuel 24.1, the Lord "incited" David to sin and then punished him; but, when the author of Chronicles retells this story, he says it was "a *śāṭān*" (a role of testing or punishing that could be played by God's angelic ministers) who incited David's sin (1 Chron 21.1). Thus, the satan figure takes on the sinister side of God's character and allows him to be seen as more purely benevolent. At first, the satans and spirits that are used to absolve God are still seen as ministers under divine authority,[207] but they slowly become more and more autonomous, which further distances God from their increasingly dreadful deeds:[208] satan figures go from being God's servants to being his enemies. And, to explain the great evils of the world, power is concentrated in a particular individual with cosmic authority, legions of demons, and a desire to take God's place: "Satan" is born.

According to Ryan Stokes, this process was nearly complete by the end of the first century. The New Testament presents vestiges of Satan's old role as God's "disciplinary emissary," but it sees him primarily as God's enemy, and this sets the stage for "the exclusion of any notion of the Satan as a functionary of God," even though hints of it continue in the second century and beyond.[209] Similarly, Kurt Flasch says that, in the New Testament, Satan is near the apex of his rise to power but has not quite reached it, for he still cannot act without God's permission.[210] Archie Wright allows more prominence for the idea of Satan as God's minister in the New Testament, and this is consistent with a number of studies, including that of Isaac Soon[211] and Emma Wasserman.[212] But Wright would seem to agree with Flasch that the definitive "shift in theological understanding" was imminent: the Apostolic and early Christian Fathers discarded the notion of Satan's functioning "under [divine] authority and sovereignty" and created the "autonomous or semiautonomous evil figure" of later Christianity.[213] For Henry Ansgar Kelly, the New Testament is fairly consistent with earlier Jewish writings in its presentation of Satan

---

[206] Flasch, *Le Diable*, 25–26, 28; Wright, *Satan*, 151; Russell, "Historical Satan," 41–42.
[207] Wright, *Satan*, 3, 246; Flasch, *Le Diable*, 63; Theißen, "Monotheismus," 50.
[208] Compare Wright, *Satan*, 3.
[209] Stokes, *The Satan*, 210, 22–23. But Stokes's book lacks sweeping statements about Satan's role in theodicy.
[210] Flasch, *Le Diable*, 63.
[211] Soon, *Disabled Apostle*, 68–81.
[212] Wasserman, *Apocalypse*.
[213] Wright, *Satan*, 250–51.

as a "chief minister of God Himself ... responsible for testing the virtue of humankind." But Kelly, too, thinks that Christians quickly abandoned this Biblical view in favor of the patristic "Satan who rebelled against God as Lucifer, and became God's enemy."[214] Kelly is thinking primarily of Origen, whose belief that Satan fell before the creation of humanity "had the effect of making Satan much, much worse than he originally was seen to be." According to Kelly, this "turned Christianity into a highly dualistic religion, with the Principle of Good on one side and a powerful Principle of Evil on the other side."[215] Jeffrey Russell takes the more moderate position that patristic authors, developing an element they had inherited from Judaism, "departed from the original pre-Christian monism" and "moved in the direction of dualism." They "stopped," however, "well and emphatically short of the pure dualistic view." Russell seems to regard this movement as a long, slow process that reached its fullness by the fifth century.[216] Burns favorably cites Russell, seeing even more continuity between the post-exilic Jewish vision and that of second- and third-century Christianity.[217]

Those who see a patristic shift toward dualism point to the struggle against Marcion and the Gnostics, where we see the ultimate expression of Satan's rise to power.[218] Here, the satan figure has become so powerful that he is the Demiurge (Creator) and rightful ruler of this world who accounts for all the perceived evil in creation, Scripture, and the human experience, allowing the Father of Jesus (or the high Gnostic deity) to be a God of supreme and untouchable goodness and transcendence. According to some scholars, this challenged patristic authors to accentuate the power and independence of the satan figure in their own efforts to better explain evil and to provide an orthodox alternative to the Demiurge.[219] Of course, Christians had to be careful that this powerful Satan did not become the Demiurge, so they emphasized that he was not evil by nature but was the good creation of God who had fallen due to the misuse of free will.

Thus, scholars argue that the emphasis on Satan as a fallen creature is an effort to limit the power of Satan in order to defend monotheism.[220] Gerd Theißen connects this to other efforts to defend monotheism

---

[214] Kelly, *Satan*, 163–70.
[215] Kelly, *Satan*, 142–45.
[216] Russell, *Satan*, 219.
[217] Burns, *Did God Care?*, 135–36, 149, 196–269.
[218] Russell, "Historical Satan," 42–43; Theißen, "Monotheismus."
[219] Wright, *Satan*, 233.
[220] Russell, "Historical Satan," 43; Russell, *Satan*, 219–20.

that he thinks began even in Second Temple Judaism and first-century Christianity. These include (1) avoiding references to Satan altogether, (2) representing him as merely a negative psychological force in the human person, and (3) emphasizing that God crushed him at the cross and/or will definitively crush him in an eschatological battle.[221] But why does Theißen not include the idea that God uses Satan's evil actions to play a role in his plan? When New Testament authors indicated that Satan's most heinous crime (his attack upon Christ) only served to bring about the salvation of the world and the exaltation of Christ,[222] did this not show that Satan's power is no threat to God?

The reason, I think, that Theißen and many other authors do not mention this is that, according to the grand narrative outlined earlier, the idea that God uses Satan as his minister is supposed to be fading away. Scholars such as Stokes recognize that the idea of Satan as God's enemy often coexists in the same text with the idea of Satan as God's minister, but there is a basic assumption that the two ideas are ultimately incompatible: to the extent that Satan is God's minister, he cannot (it is thought) function as a theodicy. But is this true? Does the fact that Satan at the crucifixion was bringing about God's foreordained plan make God responsible for his Son's death? Some have thought so, but the impact of the story would surely be different if it were *God the Father* who was said to enter Judas and to put it into his heart to betray Jesus.

Sydney Page is right to argue that there is, perhaps, tension, but no conflict in Scripture between "Satan as an implacable enemy of God" and Satan as his "servant." Whether Satan acts by divine permission or "as an unwitting instrument," his actions fall "under the overarching sovereignty of God."[223] Similarly, Wasserman has recently and compellingly argued that the desire for theodicy through dualism is not as prominent in pseudepigraphal and New Testament writings as the "strong scholarly consensus" has assumed and that the angelic rebels in these texts remain "powerless noncompetitors" subordinate to the supreme God.[224] Cato Gulaker, too, thinks that the "subordination of agents of evil to monistic cosmology" is clearly dominant.[225]

The present study will show that this preservation of divine supremacy is crystal clear even in Tertullian and Origen, who simultaneously regard

---

[221] Theißen, "Monotheismus," 50–58; Russell, "Historical Satan," 43.
[222] Pagels, "Social History," Part II, 17–18.
[223] Page, "Satan," 449n2, 65.
[224] Wasserman, *Apocalypse*, Chapter 2, including 107 and 140.
[225] Gulaker, *Satan*, 4–15.

Satan as a malicious enemy and a divine minister. In fact, I suggest that Tertullian and Origen's greater emphasis on Satan as God's enemy corresponded to a greater emphasis on Satan's subordination to God, which kept him from threatening divine supremacy. As we shall see, Origen used Satan as a theodicy, blaming actions on him that some would have attributed to God; but, these actions were providentially folded into the divine plan.

With the exception of Burns, the scholarly recognition of this has been minimal. The topic does not appear at all in Kelly's multiple chapters on patristic literature; and Wright only briefly (but insightfully) mentions that Tertullian sees Satan "like the Destroying Angel of YHWH … who carries out the opposite of what God is doing in the world but with God's permission."[226] Flasch correctly observes that one of Origen's responses to Celsus is that Satan is no threat to God's supremacy because he serves God's purposes.[227] Russell's references to Satan working under divine permission in Tertullian and Origen are fuller; but, he attaches minimal importance to the idea and focuses on the created nature of Satan as the patristic defense against dualism.[228] As already noted, Burns more explicitly acknowledges that Origen and others inherited (in Burns' terminology) the "attenuated dualism" of Judaism in which demonic powers distance God somewhat from evil while still being kept within a monotheistic framework of divine direction.[229] I agree with this, though I question the appropriateness of the phrase "attenuated dualism." Based on the prominence of the idea of Satan as God's agent in Tertullian and Origen, I hope to show that the supposed second- or third-century patristic creation of an independent Satan posited by some scholars did not happen.

With this framework in place, we are ready to consider the Jewish and early Christian tradition of God's use of evil powers, which Tertullian and Origen, contrary to the general view, inherited and adapted.

2.2 Superhuman Punishing Agents

Based on etymology and narrative context, scholars claim that the noun *śāṭān* in the Hebrew Bible, whether used of a human or superhuman, referred to the role of an "adversary," "accuser," "persecutor,"[230] or,

---

[226] Wright, *Satan*, 231, 33; Russell, *Satan*, 94.
[227] *Cels.* 6.42–44 (SC 147:278–90); Flasch, *Le Diable*, 77–79.
[228] Russell, *Satan*, 92–98, 133–34, 219–20; Russell, "Historical Satan," 42–45.
[229] Burns, *Did God Care?*, 135–36, 49.
[230] Wright, *Satan*, 12–17, 49; Page, "Satan," 449; Hamori, "Early History," 82.

in Stokes argument, "executioner" of wrongdoers.[231] Regardless of the precise meaning of the word, Stokes and others make a good case that a *śāṭan* often functioned to punish the wicked on behalf of a superior.[232] For support, Stokes points to the earliest use of *śāṭan* to refer to a superhuman being in Numbers 22.[233] Here, God's "anger" burns against the wicked Balaam, and "the angel of YHWH" stands "in the way as his *śāṭan*" with a drawn sword, ready to slay him for his perversity.[234] The "angel of YHWH" plays a similar role in the accounts of David's census,[235] where he is "the destroying angel"[236] with a drawn sword who kills seventy thousand Israelites as a punishment for David's (and perhaps for the Israelites') sin. Stokes thinks that the Chronicler intends this Destroyer to be the same as the *śāṭan* mentioned at the beginning of his account;[237] and Page notes that the Targum of Chronicles identifies this *śāṭan* as God's agent.[238]

The conclusion from these passages is that the noun *śāṭan* (when not used of a human) originally referred to the angel of YHWH when he was playing the role of an executioner of sinners. This was not an uncommon role for angelic beings: according to Exodus 12.23, God killed the firstborn of the sinful Egyptians by the agency of "the Destroyer" (*hammašḥît*); and Psalm 78.49–50 says that he accomplished the last plague when "He let loose on them his fierce anger, wrath, indignation, and distress, a company of destroying angels" (*mal'ăkê rāʿîm*).[239] In 2 Kings 19.35 and Isaiah 37.36, the "angel of the LORD" saves Judah from the wicked Assyrians by killing a hundred and eighty-five thousand soldiers in one night.[240]

While Numbers 22 and 1 Chron 21.1 refer to "a *śāṭan*" (without the definite article), Stokes notes that the later accounts of Zechariah 3.1–2 and the prologue of Job (which he believes contains relatively late material) refer to "the *śāṭan*." The word has come to designate, not a role of the angel of YHWH, but a particular office of "executioner" in the heavenly court.[241] In 2 Samuel 19.20–23, when the military leader Abishai wants to execute Shimei for crimes he committed against King David, David rebukes him for becoming "my *śāṭan*" and assures Shimei that he will not

---

[231] Stokes, *The Satan*, 5–25; Stokes, "Satan."
[232] Thornton, "Satan: God's Agent"; Kelly, *Satan*, Introduction.
[233] Stokes, *The Satan*, 10–11.
[234] Num 22.22, 23, 31–33.
[235] 2 Sam 24.16, 1 Chron 21.12.
[236] 1 Chron 21.15.
[237] Stokes, *The Satan*, 25n42.
[238] Wright, *Satan*, 19; Page, "Satan," 455n27; McIvor, *Targum*, 114.
[239] Stokes, *The Satan*, 119n16.
[240] Stokes, *The Satan*, 27.
[241] Ibid.

die. According to Stokes, Zechariah 3.1–2 describes a similar situation in the heavenly realm: like Abishai, "the *śāṭan*" is a functionary of the divine King who wants to execute a transgressor (the High Priest Joshua) for his sin, but the divine King intercedes.[242]

According to Stokes, "the *śāṭan*" in the prologue of Job is a similar functionary. In this passage, God removes the hedge of protection that typically prevents "the *śāṭan*" from harming a righteous person. The implication is that there is no hedge of protection around the wicked and that the Satan's normal activity involves afflicting them and killing them. Stokes believes that he was "authorized" to do this as an executioner "on behalf of God."[243] This idea may be supported by the fact that even the Satan's anomalous attacks on the righteous Job appear to be in keeping with God's will. As proof that the Satan is acting as God's agent, Page notes that the "hand" of God and the "hand" of the Satan by which Job is struck are interchangeable.[244] Job says that it is "God" from whom he has received "the bad" (Job 2.10).

By the time of the Book of Jubilees (second century BC), a satan figure (the Prince of Mastema) appears for the first time as the leader of "evil spirits." Jubilees is following the Book of the Watchers (third century BC), in which these evil spirits are the spawn of the superhuman beings who descend and mate with human women in Genesis 6.2–4.[245] It is important to note that, in the Hebrew Bible, the function of evil spirits is somewhat comparable to that of a *śāṭan*. As Esther J. Hamori observes, YHWH's punishment of the wicked sometimes involves sending a "spirit" (*rûaḥ*) "as a divine agent" who brings about "destructive justice by means of falsehood."[246] In Judges 9.22, God sends "an evil spirit" between the murderous ruler Abimelech and his wicked supporters, which results in treachery and slaughter. 1 Samuel repeatedly speaks of the "evil spirit from YHWH/God" that tormented the disobedient King Saul.[247] In 1 Kings 22.19–23 and 2 Chronicles 18:18–22, God commissions a spirit who offers to lie to the prophets of Ahab and entice the wicked king to fight a battle in which he meets his death. In 2 Kings 19.7 and Isaiah 37.7, God puts "a spirit" in the wicked Assyrian king Sannacherib that causes him to

---

[242] Stokes, *The Satan*, 11–17, compare 8.
[243] Stokes, *The Satan*, 41.
[244] Page, "Satan," 451–52, re: Job 1.11–12, 2.4, 2.10.
[245] *Jub.* 10.3–6, 48 (trans. by VanderKam, 42–43, 157–59); 1 Enoch 6–9, 15–16, 19.1 (trans. by Nickelsburg and VanderKam, 23–27, 36–39); Stokes, *The Satan*, 81, 184.
[246] Hamori, "Spirit," 18.
[247] 1 Sam 16.14, 15, 16, 23; 18.10, 19.9.

return home and die by the sword. In Jubilees, "evil spirits" fulfill a similar role, but they act under the direction of the Prince of Mastema, who says that he needs them "to exercise the authority of my will among humanity. For they are meant for (the purpose of) destroying and misleading before my punishment because the evil of humanity is great."[248] In Jubilees' retelling of Exodus, these evil spirits are the agents who kill the firstborn of Egypt in the last plague.[249]

In Jubilees, we find that the role of evil spirits in punishing sinners is bound up with their commission to rule the wicked nations of the earth. The explanation for this is probably that these evil spirits are envisioned (in keeping with the Book of Watchers) as the progeny of the "sons of God"[250] in Genesis 6.2–4, who fell by joining themselves with human women. Thus, these evil spirits were associated with other traditions about the "sons of God."[251] And, according to the most important of these traditions, when God "divided humankind" (at the Tower of Babel), he gave each nation its inheritance and fixed its boundaries, "according to the number of the sons of God" (Deut 32.8–9 – translated as "sons of God" or "angels of God" in the LXX).[252] This indicated that God had appointed a "son of God" to govern each nation.

The nations, however, were often hostile to Israel; and their gods were identified as *šēdîm* (translated with δαιμόνια in the LXX), false gods whose worship made YHWH jealous and who desired the blood of human children.[253] I am not arguing that the false gods of the nations (*šēdîm*/δαιμόνια) were explicitly identified as the "sons of God"[254] who ruled the nations by divine appointment, but one can see how ancient Jews might have concluded that the "sons of God," like the *šēdîm*, were wicked and responsible for wickedness among the people they ruled (cf. Dan 10.13, 20–21).[255] In light of this, it makes sense that the Book of Watchers

---

[248] *Jub.* 10:8 (trans. by VanderKam, 43); Stokes, *The Satan*, 88, 92; Forsyth, *Old Enemy*, 185–86.
[249] *Jub.* 49.2 (trans. by VanderKam, 160).
[250] Hebrew: *bĕnê [hā]ʾĕlōhîm*; Gk in LXX οἱ υἱοὶ τοῦ θεοῦ.
[251] See Ps 89.6–7; Job 1–2; Dan 3.25, 28.
[252] Translation of the New Revised Standard Catholic Edition modified; Stokes, *The Satan*, 59. On this phrase in the Masoretic Text and the LXX, see Wasserman, *Apocalypse*, 61n5.
[253] Deut 32.16–17; Ps 106.36–38; Stokes, *The Satan*, 51–52.
[254] Sometimes translated as "angels" in the LXX and the Greek of 1 Enoch 19.1–2. On 1 Enoch 19.1–2, see Wasserman, *Apocalypse*, 71.
[255] Dale B. Martin ("When Did Angels Become Demons?") argues that, before the second or third century AD, no one thought of δαιμόνια (the gentile gods) and ἄγγελοι as the same species; but Wasserman (*Apocalypse*, 114, 123) observes that a "subset of polemical literature ... works to recast the gods of others as bit players in the lesser ranks of the divine kingdom."

and Jubilees took the lustful sons of God in Genesis 6 as the source of evil practices and violence on the earth, and presented the evil spirits they produced either as the instigators of the worship of false gods[256] or as the false gods (δαιμόνια) themselves.[257] At the same time, as the offspring of the Sons of God in Deuteronomy 32.8–9, these spirits were seen as ruling the nations by divine appointment.[258] And this divine appointment became associated with God's commission of satan figures and evil spirits to punish the wicked. Thus, we can see how these figures came to be seen in the later tradition as simultaneously the rightful rulers of the wicked, the source of wickedness, and the punishers of wickedness.

This theme is apparent a century after Jubilees in some of the documents of the Dead Sea Scrolls (c. first century BC). In the *Damascus Document*, the satan figure Belial and his angels seem to be authorized to deceive and inspire wickedness among the nations; but they also carry out God's anger at apostate Jews: "strength and might and great anger with fiery flames are in the han[d] of all the angels of destruction against those who rebel against the way and despise the statute."[259] Similarly, in the *War Scroll*, Belial and his spirits counsel the nations they rule with "evil and wickedness," but they appear to serve as God's agents of "destruction."[260] In the *Rule of the Community*, the Angel of Darkness and his spirits inspire and rule over the sins of the faithful, administering "punishments" "in compliance with [God's] instructions," and the Levites ask the Lord to "hand over" the wicked to "those carrying out acts of vengeance."[261] As Cato Gulaker observes, we see here "the subordination of agents of evil to a monistic cosmology."[262]

In some of the writings of the New Testament, Satan is "the ruler" or "god of this world order."[263] By sinning, people become sons or slaves of the devil and of sin,[264] members of a demonic kingdom opposed to God.[265]

---

[256] 1 Enoch 7–8, 15–16 (trans. by Nickelsburg and VanderKam, 24–26, 36–38).
[257] *Jub.* 7.27, 11.5, 15.31–32 (trans. by VanderKam, 35, 47, 61); compare Stokes, *The Satan*, 97.
[258] Wasserman, *Apocalypse*, 90–91.
[259] 4QD^a 2:5–7, 8.1–2 (trans. by Fraade, 34, 60); Stokes, *The Satan*, 157.
[260] 1QM 13.9–12, 14.9–10 (trans. by Martínez, 108–9). For discussion, see Wasserman, *Apocalypse*, 104–5.
[261] 1QS 2.5–6, 3.13–23 (trans. by Martínez, 4, 6). For discussion, see Wasserman, *Apocalypse*, 94–97.
[262] Gulaker, *Satan*, 9.
[263] John 12.31, 14.30, 16.11; 1 Cor 2.6–8; 2 Cor 4.4; Eph 2.1–3; Farrar, "Intimate and Ultimate," 522n20.
[264] John 8.34; Rom 7.14.
[265] Acts 26.18; Luke 11.18–21; 2 Cor 6.14–15.

And yet one might conclude that he holds this position by divine appointment (Luke 4.6); and sinners can be consigned to him for discipline sanctioned by God. Wasserman observes that Paul envisions Satan, Beliar, and the Destroyer "as punishing operatives of the supreme deity," and Gulaker says something similar.[266] Paul encourages the Corinthians "to hand over" an incestuous man "to Satan for the destruction of his flesh, in order that his spirit may be saved" (1 Cor 5.5). Similarly, 1 Timothy 1.20 refers to the handing over of "shipwrecked" Christians to Satan that they may be taught not to blaspheme.[267] In addition, God seems to direct, at some level, the lies and judgment imposed by Satan and "the Lawless One" upon sinners in 2 Thessalonians 2.11–12.[268] In Revelation 9.1–11, "Apollyon," "the angel of the abyss," is the "king" of the locusts with the sting of scorpions, to whom it is "granted" (presumably by God) to "torture" (but not to kill) people who lack "the seal of God" for five months.[269]

2.3 Superhuman Testing Agents

We have just seen that Satan and his evil spirits, ironically, inspire (or tempt) people to sin as well as punishing them for it and that this temptation somehow falls under divine direction. Although this topic is not our focus, it requires brief consideration. In the prologue of Job, God allows Satan to afflict a righteous man. Satan's intent is to reveal his fickleness or cause him to be unfaithful, while God's intent is to prove his faithfulness. This began an important tradition of Satan as a divinely sanctioned instrument of testing. According to the scholarly consensus, the rewritten version of the sacrifice of Isaac in Jubilees imitates the story of Job.[270] In the original story, God tests Abraham by asking him to sacrifice his long-awaited son; but, in Jubilees, it is the Prince of Mastema who calls into question Abraham's faithfulness and challenges God to test it. Abraham passes the test, putting Mastema to shame, and the angel of the Lord steps in at the last moment to save Isaac from death.

The Joban model is particularly prominent in the New Testament, which often indicates that the devil's temptation of the righteous is, as Page says, "under God's sovereign control."[271] In 2 Corinthians 12.7–9,

---

[266] Wasserman, *Apocalypse*, 138; Gulaker, *Satan*, 9–11.
[267] Thornton, "Satan as Adversary"; Kelly, *Satan*, 36–40; Wright, *Satan*, 175, 79.
[268] Kelly, *Satan*, 90–92; Forsyth, *Old Enemy*, 281.
[269] Compare Gulaker, *Satan*, 159, 198, 226n181.
[270] Stokes, *The Satan*, 81, 99n13.
[271] Page, "Satan," 456–65.

Paul complains of a "thorn in the flesh," which he identifies as "an angel of Satan" who "harasses" him. And yet this thorn "was given" to him, presumably by God,[272] to keep him in a state of humility and dependence.[273] When Paul prays for its removal, God tells him, "My grace is enough for you."[274] In Luke 22.31–32, Satan is said to have "demanded" permission to "winnow" the disciples during Jesus' passion. He hopes the threat of torture and death will cause the disciples to desert Jesus and show their half-hearted loyalty; but, Jesus prays that Simon's faith will not fail.[275]

Aspects of Jesus' own passion resonate with the story of Job. It occurred through evil people at the prompting of the devil;[276] but, the Father and the Son allowed the devil to act, because his hostility carried out a divine plan: the "cup" of the passion was the Father's "will."[277] Jesus in the Gospel of John willingly chooses to suffer "just as the Father has commanded me";[278] and he even encourages Judas to act quickly (John 13.27). "The ruler of this world" has no power over Jesus, but Jesus lets him have his way (John 14.30–31). Similarly, Pilate's authority over Jesus' life was "given to [him] from above" (John 19.11). The Father "did not spare his own Son" (Rom 8.32), who was "handed over according to the fixed plan and foreknowledge of God" (Acts 2.23). The idea that Satan's evil attack on Christ was directed by God appears with regard to the martyrs. In Revelation 2.10 Christ tells the church at Smyrna, "the devil is going to throw some of you into prison"; but he says that the purpose of this is "to test you"; and he encourages the victims, "Be faithful to the point of death, and I will give you the crown of life."[279]

In the New Testament, the devil sometimes tests people with the carrot of pleasure rather than the stick of pain. The archetype is Jesus' temptation by the devil in the wilderness.[280] The famished Jesus is tempted with food, pride, and power, but he remains blameless (cf. Heb 4.15).[281] Significantly, this temptation was God's will: Jesus was led "by the Spirit to be tempted by the devil" (Matt 4.1). In keeping with this, the prayer

---

[272] Soon, *Disabled Apostle*, 69–73.
[273] Page, "Satan," 464–65.
[274] See the excellent analysis in Soon *Disabled Apostle*, 73–81.
[275] Page, "Satan," 459.
[276] Acts 2.22–23; Luke 22.22, 22.53; John 13.2, 13.27.
[277] Matt 26.39; Luke 22.42.
[278] John 12.27, 14.30–31.
[279] Although he is "the antagonist," Satan is "serving God's purposes" (Gulaker, *Satan*, 71–72).
[280] Matt 4.1–11; Mark 1.12–13; Luke 4.1–13.
[281] Page, "Satan," 456–57.

requesting that God not lead Christians into temptation but to deliver them from the Evil One[282] may imply, Page observes, that he often "uses Satan as an instrument" of temptation.[283]

2.4 Human Punishing Agents

Studies of Satan as God's minister of punishment rarely discuss the related (and important) idea of evil nations and kings as God's ministers of punishment. Page (in a brief comment)[284] and especially Wasserman's insightful analysis are exceptions.[285] We have seen that, from the time of Jubilees, there was a growing association of Satan and wicked nations;[286] and this expressed itself in the New Testament passages just considered, which identify persecution perpetrated by sinful magistrates as the actions of Satan (e.g. Rev 2.10). For our purpose, a very brief and nonchronological summary of the theme of wicked nations as God's servants is sufficient.

According to the Jewish Scriptures, YHWH reigns over the nations.[287] This means that he can remove kings and set them up.[288] Those who oppose him inspire his laughter (Ps 2.1–4), for they are like "a drop from a bucket" (Isa 40.15, 23), earthen vessels in the hands of the divine potter. And one of God's main uses for these nations is to chastise the people of Israel when they sin.[289] God gave Israel "over to plunderers" and "sold them into the power of their enemies" (Judg 2.13–14). The idea that God uses hostile nations to discipline his people appears most dramatically in prophetic reflections on Assyria and Babylon. God says, "Ah, Assyria, the rod of my anger .... Against a godless nation I send him ... to take spoil and seize plunder" (Isa 10.5–6). This does not mean that Assyria is conscious of being God's servant: "this is not what he intends, nor does he have this in mind" (Isa 10.7). He thinks that he has conquered the nations by his own strength (Isa 10.13). He is like an axe that "vaunt[s] itself over the one who wields it" or like a "saw [that] magnif[ies] itself against the one who handles it" (Isa 10.15). And so, when the Lord has finished using him to punish Israel and threaten Jerusalem, "he will punish the arrogant boasting of the king of Assyria" and decimate his warriors with sickness

---

[282] Luke 11.2–4; Matt 6.9–13.
[283] Page, "Satan," 458–59.
[284] Page, "Satan," 449n2.
[285] Wasserman, *Apocalypse*, 62–64, 83.
[286] Compare Wasserman, *Apocalypse*, 115.
[287] Deut 10.17–18; Ps 22.28, 47.7–8, 113.4–8.
[288] Dan 2.21, 4.17, 4.25; Ps 2.8.
[289] Lev 26.21, 25, 33, 41.

(Isa 10.12, 16). Similarly, God is said to use the wicked Babylonians as his "servant" to punish Judah (Jer 25.9), though in the end he will also "punish" them "for their iniquity" and their plundering.[290]

2.5 Punishing Agents in Greek Religion

Before considering the reception of Jewish ideas about punishing agents in second- and third-century Christianity, we should briefly explore comparable ideas in the Hellenistic tradition. Hesiod (c. seventh century BC) indicates that Zeus has agents (δαίμονες one infers from other passages) to afflict the wicked with famine, plague, and defeat. These immortal "guards" are "clothed in mist, roaming back and forth over the whole earth, watching for judgements and heartless deeds" that merit divine vengeance (ὄπιν). In conjunction with these, the virgin goddess Justice (Δίκη) sits beside her father, Zeus, and reminds him of the wickedness of magistrates and rulers until he makes their people pay the penalty.[291]

Hesiod's punitive demons are similar to the Erinyes (Furies) described perhaps two centuries later in Aeschylus' *Oresteia* (c. 458 BC). The Erinyes relentlessly torment Orestes and try to take vengeance on him for killing his mother, even though she killed his father.[292] At first, the Erinyes will not accept Orestes' divine acquittal and decide to poison the whole community; but, Athena's threats and arguments convince them to relent and to become enforcers of justice rather than blood-for-blood vengeance.[293] References to the Erinyes appear as late as the second or third century AD. These dreadful snake-haired beings are the "eye" of Justice: they inspect the peoples of the earth and punish them for their base deeds. And yet perhaps respectful hymns will make them softhearted.[294] Algra refers to the Erinyes and punishing demons of the Greek tradition as a "spiritual police force,"[295] but the tradition seems to nuance both the justice of their punishments and their obedience to the gods.

2.6 Demonic "Executioners"

Keeping in mind this Hellenistic tradition, we can turn to consider how Christians in the second and third centuries received the concept of Satan and demons as divine agents of punishment in Scripture and related

---

[290] Jer 25.12, 14; Hab 1.11, 1.13, 2.8. See also 2 Macc 6.13, 7.18–19.
[291] *Op.* 122–24, 238–69 (West, *Hesiod*, 100–1, 106–8).
[292] *Choephori* 1048–62 (Garvie, 45–46).
[293] *Eumenides* 778–1047 (West, *Aeschyli Eumenides*, 44–57).
[294] *Orphic Hymns* 69–70 (Malamis, 98–100).
[295] Algra, "Stoics," 75.

writings. At first, there is very little to report. The Shepherd of Hermas refers to an "angel of vengeance (τιμωρίας)." This sounds like Satan, since the author says that God hands over sinners to this angel for discipline and purification through sickness, loss, and terrible tortures (cf. 1 Cor 5.5); but, significantly, the author is speaking about one "of the righteous angels."[296] Athenagoras says that Satan was originally an angel entrusted with administering material things; but, now that he has fallen, he neglects his work and acts wickedly.[297] In general, Christian authors of the second century see persecution, like Christ's passion, as a work of Satan that is, presumably, under God's control. And yet these authors show almost no direct engagement with Scriptural passages on Satan and his evil spirits as ministers of punishment. In contrast, in the third century, Tertullian engages with many of these passages, and Origen engages with nearly all of them.[298] In fact, they both use the term "executioner" (Gk δήμιος; Lt *carnifex*) as an analogy for wicked demons that punish sinners by divine direction.[299] This analogy continues to be used, appearing in Eusebius,[300] John Chrysostom,[301] and Augustine.[302]

The term "executioner" (Gk δήμιος; Lt *carnifex*) was never a translation of the Hebrew *śāṭan*, which the Greek Septuagint typically translates as διάβολος (usually thought to mean "slanderer" or "adversary"). In the Septuagint, δήμιος is only used in 2 Maccabees, where it refers to despicable rulers (e.g. 2 Macc 7.29). As just noted, the idea that Satan punishes sinners on God's behalf is based (especially in Origen) on many of the Biblical passages reviewed earlier; but, this does not necessarily mean that the analogical use of the term δήμιος/*carnifex* derives from Scriptural exegesis.

In the ancient mediterranean world, a reference to the "executioner" conjured up horrible images, for it was his job to execute criminals and to extract information and confessions through cutting, tearing, stretching, and burning – often displayed publicly.[303] Such a person would have to be, or become, despicable. According to Cicero, ancient Romans were so

---

[296] *Pastor Hermae*, Similitudo 6.3 (63) (GCS 48:61); Wright, *Satan*, 218–19.
[297] *Legatio pro Christianis* 24.2–3 (Marcovich, 79–81); Burns, *Did God Care?*, 120–22.
[298] Clement's engagement is minimal.
[299] For example, Tertullian, *Fug.* 2.6–7 (Marra, 63).
[300] *Comm. Isa.* 1.65–67 (GCS 60:94–100).
[301] *De diabolo tentatore homiliae* 1.4 (SC 560:140–42); *In principium actorum* 3.4–6 (PG 51:95).
[302] *De diversis questionibus LXXXIII*, 53.1–4 (CCSL 44A:85–91); *Enarrat. Ps.* 77, 26–28 (CSEL 95.3:224–28).
[303] Clark, "Desires of the Hangman"; Cook, "Envisioning the Panoply."

disturbed by the *carnifex* that they made him live outside the city, deprived of fresh air and light.³⁰⁴ At the same time, the cruelty of the *carnifex* served a good and necessary function by discouraging crime and ensuring the safety of the community. Gillian Clark points out Augustine's compelling description: "What is more loathsome than an executioner? What is crueler or more frightening than that soul? But even in the laws he has a necessary place, and he is integrated (*inseritur*) into the order (*ordinem*) of a well-run city."³⁰⁵

The first extant analogical use of δήμιος/*carnifex* is in the works of Philo, the Jewish philosopher and exegete of Alexandria (first century AD). Although Philo generally claims that God's agents of punishment are morally good angels or humans, there is one passage in which he says that God appoints (ἐφίστησι) wicked tyrants, like public executioners (οἷα δημίους κοινούς), over violent and unjust cities to punish them. Philo's larger point is that the flourishing of wicked rulers should not make people question the existence or justice of divine providence. God will punish these tyrants, but he sometimes delays in doing so, because some "evils are not cleansed without a savage soul" (ὠμῆς γὰρ δίχα ψυχῆς οὐ καθαίρεται κακία). "In the same way," cities disapprove of the character (τὴν γνώμην) of executioners, but they support them (ἀνατρέφουσιν) because of the usefulness of their service (τὸ τῆς ὑπηρεσίας χρήσιμον).³⁰⁶

The next relevant reference appears several generations later in the work of the Middle Platonist Plutarch. Like Philo, he seems to have believed that divine agents of punishment (δαίμονες acting as τιμωροί) are all good. He is standoffish about the idea of "certain Romans" and "the philosophers who surround" the Stoic Chrysippus that "base daemons" (φαῦλα δαιμόνια), rather like the Furies (ἐρινυώδεις τινές), "go about for inspection," and that "the gods use them (χρῶνται) as executioners (δημίοις) and punishers (κολασταῖς) of irreverent and unjust people."³⁰⁷ In another passage, Plutarch accuses Chrysippus of trying to justify the suffering of righteous people by saying that it is caused, not by the gods, but by "the base daemons" they have appointed to punish the wicked.³⁰⁸ In that case, Plutarch observes, the gods would still be guilty, just as a king is guilty who appoints "bad and impulsive satraps" over a province and then overlooks

---

[304] *Pro Rabirio Perduellionis Reo* 5.15–16 (Marek, 63–64).
[305] *De ordine* 2.4 (12) (Fuhrer, 151), cited and discussed in Clark, "Desires of the Hangman," 140.
[306] *Prov.* 2.39–40, preserved in Eusebius, *Praep. ev.* 8.14 (GCS 43.1:472).
[307] *Quest. rom.* 51.276f–77a (Boulogne, 139).
[308] In fact, I think that Plutarch has misconstrued Chrysippus' argument.

their mistreatment and neglect of his best citizens."[309] These passages from Plutarch convinced M. Pohlenz that Chrysippus believed in the divine use of evil demons as agents of punishment.[310] Keimpe Algra disagrees,[311] but he does think that some Stoics believed in evil demons and imagined that their wicked actions could be incorporated into "the overall fabric of [God's] providential design."[312] Perhaps this makes sense, given the relative "monism" of Stoicism in distinction to Platonism.[313] Nienke Vos notes that, if this is true, "the Stoic description is similar to Origen's later understanding of the paradoxical synergy of providence and free will."[314]

2.7 Theological Function of Punishing Agents

We have now considered the main traditions of punishing agents that set a precedent for Origen's view, and it is time to consider the theological or polemical function(s) of these traditions. For Philo, God's use of wicked tyrants as agents of divine punishment justified the fact that God lets such people flourish, in spite of their wickedness. As we saw in Section 1, this kind of reasoning was identified by Koch in Origen, and it appears in several of his discussions of God's use of evil humans and demons. This reasoning, however, does not play an obvious role in the bulk of the material reviewed earlier. Determining what themes do emerge from this material is difficult, given its non-systematic nature, but some observations are possible. In my discussion of the grand narrative of Satan's history, I suggested that the idea of Satan as God's minister can function both as a theodicy (in the sense that God is not the actor) and as an affirmation of God's supremacy (evil is subject to divine direction). But is this apparent in the texts?

The first use (as a theodicy) may be apparent in Jubilees' retelling of the sacrifice of Isaac. By making the Prince of Mastema the instigator of the test, rather than God, the author absolves God from asking for Isaac's blood, even though everything happens by God's permission. In most other cases of God's use of evil, it is difficult to prove that theodicy is at work. The most we can say is that, if God's satanic minister is removed from the scene, the effect is disturbing. What if it were implied that God, rather than Satan, had killed Job's children? What if God, rather than

---

[309] *Stoic. rep.* 37.1051c–d (Casevitz, 74–75).
[310] Pohlenz, *Die Stoa*.
[311] Algra, "Stoics," 75.
[312] Algra, "Stoics," 88–89; Bobzien, *Determinism*, 346–49.
[313] Burns, *Did God Care?*, 103–4.
[314] Vos, "Introduction," 15–16.

"an angel of Satan," had tormented Paul with a thorn in his flesh? What if Paul had told the Corinthians to hand over the incestuous man "*to God for the destruction of his flesh*"?

The principle that God's use of evil serves to affirm his supremacy is easier to discern, both with respect to wicked humans and superhumans. For many ancient Israelites, their subjection to the brutal Assyrians who despised YHWH would have proven YHWH's impotence. But the prophets assert that Assyria is merely a clay vessel in the hands of the divine potter, to be dropped and shattered when its dirty work is done. The apparent power of the nations poses no threat to God, for their evil actions are part of his plan. Similarly, the New Testament claims that Satan's apparent victory over Jesus during his passion does not prove that Jesus is powerless, for Jesus and his Father allowed (and even encouraged) the devil to act, since he would only be carrying out the divine plan. It was this theme that the North African Christian Tertullian passionately appropriated in the early third century, and it is to this that we now turn.

2.8 Punishing Agents in Tertullian

In his treatise *Flight in Persecution*, Tertullian argued that Christians should not try to avoid martyrdom. Since iniquity is "from the devil," Tertullian writes, it would seem that the iniquity of persecution proceeds (*evenire*) from the devil, who carries it out. But the devil can only persecute when the "right" (*ius*) is "granted to him" (*conceditur ei*) by God. He could not have tempted Job "unless he had received power from God," nor could he have "winnowed" the disciples at Christ's passion without "permission" (re: Luke 22.31–32).[315]

In fact, God does more than give permission: it is really from him that persecution proceeds (*eveniat*).[316] The "will of God" is the true reason (*ratio*): "the iniquity of the devil [merely] follows as the instrument (*instrumentum*) of persecution." The devil is not in charge: his service (*ministerium*) fulfills God's decision (*arbitrium*).[317] The request in the *Pater noster* that God not "lead us into temptation" but "rescue us from the Evil One" proves that God is ultimately in charge of temptation and that he merely uses the devil for his purpose.[318] The prophets identify God as the one who "makes evil" (re: Isa 45.7), who will "bring to life" and "kill" (re: Deut 32.39), who "will

---

[315] *Fug.* 1.2, 2.1, 2.3–4, 2.7 (Marra, 58–63).
[316] *Fug.* 4.1 (Marra, 66).
[317] *Fug.* 2.1–2 (Marra, 60–61).
[318] *Fug.* 2.5 (Marra, 62).

refine" people like gold (re: Zech 13.9); but God does all of this through the "flaming darts of the devil" (re: Eph 6.16).[319] "Therefore," Tertullian concludes, "we believe that persecution happens *through* the Devil, but perhaps not *by* him."[320] It occurs only when God "wills" it.[321]

Tertullian identifies three reasons that God gives the devil the right to persecute.[322] The first is to test the faithful[323] and so to "distinguish between the wheat of the martyrs and the chaff of the deniers." God is like the master of athletic games (*agonotheta*), who gives a crown of approval to some and rejects others.[324] The fact that persecution promotes good things such as the fear of God, and hence true Christian belief, shows that it "cannot be credited to the devil."[325]

Second, God uses persecution to condemn sinners (*reprobationis*). In this case, "a sinner is handed over (*traditur*) to [Satan] as to an executioner" (*quasi carnifici*). According to Tertullian, this is what was happening when "the Spirit of the Lord departed from Saul, and an evil spirit from the Lord began harassing and strangling him" (re: 1 Sam 16.14). Similarly, Paul "handed Phigellus and Hermogenes over to Satan to chastise them in order that they might not blaspheme" (re: 1 Tim 1.20).[326] In *Modesty*, Tertullian argues that the sinners handed over to Satan by the Apostle, both here and in 1 Corinthians 5.5, suffered death and damnation.[327]

Finally, sometimes Satan is "permitted" by God to inflict "trials of the flesh" upon holy people in order "to humble" them and to perfect their "strength of resistance" through the experience of "weakness." This happened to Paul, who "was given an angel of Satan as a thorn to lash him" (re: 2 Cor 12.7–9).[328] According to Tertullian, all three of the scenarios he has outlined occur during persecutions, "since at that time most of all we are approved or condemned, humiliated or corrected."[329]

As we have seen, Tertullian's main point throughout is that God (not Satan) is the author of persecution. For Tertullian, this means that (1) Christians *cannot* escape persecution and (2) they *should not* escape it,

---

[319] *Fug.* 3.1–2 (Marra, 64–65).
[320] *Fug.* 2.2 (Marra, 61); Barnes, *Tertullian*, 179.
[321] *Fug.* 1.3, 2.1, 4.1 (Marra, 58, 60–61, 66–67). The Satan of Tertullian has been compared to the Destroying Angel of the Old Testament: Wright, *Satan*, 231, 33; Russell, *Satan*, 94.
[322] Russell, *Satan*, 97.
[323] *Fug.* 1.3, 2.7 (Marra, 58, 63).
[324] *Fug.* 1.3–5 (Marra, 58–59).
[325] *Fug.* 1.5–6 (Marra, 59–60).
[326] *Fug.* 2.7 (Marra, 63–64).
[327] *Pud.* 13.15–22 (CCSL 2:1305–6).
[328] *Fug.* 2.7 (Marra, 64).
[329] *Fug.* 3.1 (Marra, 64).

since all God's plans are good.³³⁰ Clearly, Tertullian uses the idea of Satan as God's minister, not as a theodicy to distance God from suffering and injustice, but to affirm his control over it. In fact, for Tertullian, to say that God uses evil is close to saying that he does evil. One is reminded of the prophetic claim that Assyria is merely a pawn in the divine hand. It is an encouraging message in the sense that nothing can threaten God's good plan; but, on the other hand, God's good plan coincides with the evil perpetrated by the wicked and so might feel harsh.

I suggest Tertullian's effort to closely associate God with testing and judgment is connected to his polemic against Marcion. From *Against Marcion* 5.7.2, we gather that Marcion thought the incestuous man in 1 Corinthians 5.5 had offended against the natural justice of the Demiurge and so was handed over to him. Presumably, this distanced the Father of Jesus from the harsh justice of destroying the sinner's flesh. But, for Tertullian, the fact that God (and/or Paul) used an agent of punishment does not distance them from the act of condemnation. Paul is "a herald of the condemning (*damnatoris*) God" who decrees the "destruction of the flesh." And so, Tertullian argues, this is clearly the same God as the Creator and judge of sinners in the Old Testament.³³¹ Similarly, Tertullian claims that the God who "brought to bear" the "angel of Satan" to relentlessly "torment" Paul and humble his pride (re: 2 Cor 12.7) is not the nice God of Marcion but the God who "gave power over Job's body to Satan that his virtue might be tested by infirmity."³³² A few chapters later, Tertullian notes that the Jesus of 2 Thessalonians 2.1–12 will judge people by sending a "delusion" through the Antichrist, showing that he is a God of vengeance (*vindicta*).³³³

For Tertullian, these passages in which the New Testament God uses evil powers to judge people show that he is the same as the fearful and just judge of the Old Testament. God is responsible for the judgments he has delegated to Satan. In saying this, there are hints (as noted earlier) that Tertullian is responding to Marcion's argument that the benevolent Father of Jesus is not responsible for the vengeance that he allows the Demiurge to inflict. Here we see the flexibility of the image of the divine agent: Marcion may have used it to distance God from vengeance, while Tertullian used it to associate God with vengeance.

---

³³⁰ *Fug.* 4.1 (Marra, 66).
³³¹ *Marc.* 5.7.2 (CCSL 1:682).
³³² *Marc.* 5.12.8 (CCSL 1:701); re: Job 1–2; 2 Cor 12.9.
³³³ *Marc.* 5.16.6–7 (CCSL 1:712).

If, like Wright and Kelly, one advocates a recovery of the Biblical view of God's lordship over Satan, it is hard to imagine a better expression of it than that of Tertullian. And yet, it is in the second and third centuries that these scholars think this Biblical view was lost. In Section 3, we will see how Origen used the idea of Satan as God's minister, not only to assert God's supremacy (like Tertullian), but also to distance God from evil (like Marcion).

3 Punishing Agents in Origen

After reviewing the traditions that preceded Origen, Sections 2.7 and 2.8 claimed that the idea that God works through evil agents functions primarily in two ways. First, it can function as a theodicy: one can say that things inconsistent with God's goodness or transcendence were not done directly by God but by evil beings whose actions he directs. Second, it can function to affirm God's supremacy: one can say that the evil powers that seem to challenge God are actually carrying out his plan. Tertullian exhibited the second function dramatically in the early third century, perhaps partly in opposition to Marcion, who seems to have exhibited the first function, in which the idea of punishing agents distances God from evil. This section will show that Origen exhibits both functions. It will also show how his ideas are drawn from (and sometimes imposed upon) the Scriptural tradition. We begin, however, with an overview of Origen's beliefs about the providential use of evil angels, the main categories of evil angels, and the meaning of divine punishment.

3.1 Everything Has Its Place

As we saw in the discussion of the preexistence of souls in Section 1, *First Principles* 2.1 says that the diverse types and circumstances of rational creatures were not part of God's original creation. Because preexistent intellects fell to differing degrees, God created a diverse material cosmos in which each fallen soul has a place and a role that corresponds to its sin. In its specific place and role, each soul is punished and healed, but it also serves to promote the healing of others. This role of ministering to the salvation of others is particularly true for angels,[334] who remain, nevertheless, beings on their own moral journey, capable of virtue and vice.[335] God gives an appropriate role for each category of soul, even for those who have

---
[334] *Princ.* Pref. 10 (Behr, 20).
[335] *Hom. Num.* 11.4 (SC 442:34–46); *Hom. Num.* 20.3.6–7 (SC 461:42–44).

fallen to become demons. Origen explains that this fatherly arrangement of everything "for the salvation of every creature" does not violate the free will of any. Creatures are the authors of the "diverse movements of their resolutions." But then these movements, "through the ineffable design of [God's] Word and Wisdom," are "appropriately and profitably adapted to the harmony of the one world. While some [(humans)] need help, others [(angels)] are able to help; and still others [(demons)] bring about struggles and contests for those who are making progress" in order that their worth and definitive victory might be "established through the difficulties of their afflictions."[336]

On a similar note, Origen says elsewhere that creatures become vessels of honor or "vessel<s> of shame"[337] through their own choice. But then, "through the justice and ineffable reason of his providence," God "dispenses" (*dispensat*) or "uses" not only honorable vessels, but also "evil vessels for his good work" (*uasis malis utitur Deus ad opus bonum*).[338] In God's plan, "nothing is useless or idle."[339] This does not mean that God approves of evil actions. For Origen, although "nothing occurs apart from his providence, either in heaven or on earth," "many things occur without his will."[340] We get the impression, however, that sometimes God's direction of demonic action goes beyond the ineffable management of providence. As we shall see, Origen speaks of God "permitting," "appointing," or "sending out" demons to play specific roles. But even in these cases, Origen is clear that God merely directs, but does not cause, their evil choices.

3.2 Categories of Evil Angels

The following pages will focus on this divine direction of demons, particularly with regard to the punishment (or discipline) of sinners. But first we need to briefly explore the categories of evil angels involved in this disciplinary process. Most important are the "rulers" (ἄρχοντες) of the nations. Following the tradition outlined in Section 2, Origen believed that, at the Tower of Babel, God divided the people into groups and assigned each to an angel (re: Deut 32.8–9). In Origen's vision, these angels taught

---
[336] *Princ.* 2.1.2 (Behr, 146); Daniélou, *Origène*, 220.
[337] Re: 2 Tim 2.20–21 and Rom 9.21–23.
[338] *Hom. Num.* 14.2.1 and 14.2.6 (SC 442:164–66 and 170); compare *Or.* 29.17–30.3 (GCS 3:391–95); compare *Hom. Luc.* 26.4 (SC 87:340–42).
[339] *Hom. Num.* 9.1.1 (SC 415:222).
[340] *Hom. Gen.* 3.2 (SC 7:114–16); compare *Cels.* 7.68 (SC 150:170–74).

the group assigned to them a unique language[341] and custom and led them to establish a nation in a designated part of the earth.[342] In keeping with the tradition, this arrangement was "for punishment";[343] but, of course, Origen believed this was a punishment of healing that perfectly corresponded to the sin of each nation. Through "God's judgement,"[344] each nation got what it deserved in terms of the "harshness" of the angel to whom it was "handed over" and the level of cold, drought, and wild beasts in its designated region.[345]

Origen emphasizes that these angels are not the benevolent administering *daimones* of Hellenistic imagination. They are the rulers of "this present evil world" (re: Gal 1.4). Thus, the people God hands over to their wicked rule are consigned "'to a disreputable mind' and to 'passions of dishonor' and 'to their heart's desire for uncleanness'" (re: Rom 1.24–32). But the benevolent purpose is that, "by being sated with sin, they may come to hate it."[346] Each nation suffers this bondage "until it has paid the penalty."[347] The Israelites initially escaped these bitter "treatments," for their nation belonged to God and not to an angel. But when they kept sinning, they "were abandoned" to, and eventually "snatched away" by, the harsh angelic "rulers" of other nations and so "paid the penalty" that others had paid.[348] For Origen, this situation is parallel to that of Christians who fall into serious sin and are excluded from the Church and "handed over to Satan" for disciplinary suffering.[349]

According to Origen, Christ partly came to depose these rulers and abolish the false knowledge they had taught (re: 1 Tim 6.20). To prevent this, the rulers attacked him and orchestrated the crucifixion (re: Ps 2.1–2); but Jesus defeated them at the cross, "seized" people "from the perverse power," and "presented [them] to God the Father."[350] Whenever Christians fall into serious sin, however, the rulers are able to recall them "into captivity"[351] and exact from them harsh "taxes of the flesh" (*tributa carnis*). In doing so, these "perverse" rulers nevertheless

---

[341] *Hom. Num.* 11.4.4 (SC 442:40).
[342] *Cels.* 5.30 (SC 147:90).
[343] *Cels.* 5.31 (SC 147:92); compare *Cels.* 8.33 (SC 150:246).
[344] *Hom. Jes. Nav.* 23.3 (SC 71:458–60).
[345] *Cels.* 5.30 (SC 147:90).
[346] *Cels.* 5.32 (SC 147:94).
[347] *Cels.* 5.30 (SC 147:90).
[348] *Cels.* 5.31 (SC 147:92).
[349] Re: 1 Cor 5.5 and 1 Tim 1.20.
[350] *Princ.* 3.3.2 (Behr, 402); *Hom. Luc.* 35.7 (SC 87:420); *Hom. Gen.* 9.3 (SC 7:248–52); *Cels.* 5.32 (SC 147:94).
[351] *Hom. Gen.* 9.3 (SC 7:248).

serve as God's ministers (re: Heb 1.14),[352] for their activity disciplines and purifies sinners.[353]

One of the ways national rulers try to retain their human slaves is through personal demons or "adversaries" (ἀντίδικος) – rather like anti-guardian angels.[354] If these adversaries can get people to sin, they can lead them to punishment.[355] But whether one has an "adversary," or the extent to which one is subject to one's adversary, is directed by the just providence of God, depending upon one's moral state. Both "good and opposing" angels are present at someone's birth, and which kind becomes the guardian of that person's soul is allotted by divine judgment (*iudicio*). Those born outside the Church or those living in sin are subject to Satanic angels; but, at conversion and baptism, they, like the Israelite slaves in Egypt, are rescued from these "work masters" and are assigned a good angelic helper.[356] But if they fall back into sin, "making themselves unworthy of angelic guardianship," they are once more "delivered to" angels of "dissipation" and "vengeance."[357]

According to Origen, everything that moves, from water to air to animals to stars, moves because of an indwelling soul or angel that God has appointed to govern it.[358] While good angels cause no harm and administer the beneficial processes of nature,[359] Stephen Bettencourt[360] notes that Satan and his demons have a kinship with (and control over) natural forces that "resemble evil."[361] This includes savage animals,[362] desolation, darkness, stagnation, cold, drought, crop failure, famine, and plague.[363] Thus, these demons are a natural source of punishment, harm,

---

[352] *ministeriales spiritus*.
[353] *Comm. Rom.* 9.30.1–4 (SC 555:178–82).
[354] Daniélou, *Origène*, 235–39; Muehlberger, *Angels*, 91–98; compare Leemans, "Angels," 52–53.
[355] *Hom. Luc.* 35.7 (SC 87:420), re: Luke 12.58.
[356] *Hom. Jes. Nav.* 23.3 (SC 71:460); *Hom. Exod.* 1.5 (SC 321:66); compare *Comm. Matt.* 13.28 (GCS 40:256–58).
[357] *Comm. Matt.* 13.6 (GCS 40:195), *Comm. Matt.* 14.21 (GCS 40:335); compare *Comm. Matt.* 13.26 (GCS 40:252–53); compare *Hom. Luc.* 35.3–5 (SC 87:414–18); compare *Hom. Num.* 24.3.4–5 (SC 461:180); compare Muehlberger, *Angels*, 98.
[358] *Princ.* 1.7.3 (Behr, 124); *Cels.* 8.31 (SC 150:242); *Hom. Jer.* 10.6 (SC 232:408–10); *Hom. Ps. 76* 3.2 (GCS 19NS:329–30); *Hom. Ezech.* 1.7 (SC 352:70); *Hom. Ps. 80* 2.2 (GCS 19NS:499); Perrone, "Scrittura," 184–88; Daniélou, *Origène*, 223.
[359] *Cels.* 8.32 and 8.36 (SC 150:244 and 252–54).
[360] Bettencourt, *Doctrina*, 49–50.
[361] Compare Philo, *De fuga et inventione* 74 (PAO 3:125), *De confusione linguarum* 180–82 (OAP 2:263–64).
[362] *Cels.* 4.92–93 (SC 136:414–18); compare *Hom. Lev.* 16.6.2 (SC 287:288).
[363] *Cels.* 8.31–32 (SC 150:242–44); *Hom. Gen.* 1.2 (SC 7:30); *Princ.* 2.8.3 (Behr, 228–30); compare *Hom. Ezech.* 1.14 (SC 352:90).

and suffering. They may not rule sections of the earth by God's law, but they serve God "by a divine decision (κρίσει)" as "executioners" (δήμιοι) to punish and convert sinners and to test the righteous.[364] Plague is probably the most characteristic work of these demons, and Origen associates them with sicknesses of divine judgment. In addition, we may presume that these demons were behind the cold, drought, and wild beasts that were the merited punishment of nations assigned to various rulers at the Tower of Babel.

As we can see, when Origen speaks of God punishing through demons, these demons can sometimes be placed in one of the three categories discussed earlier: "rulers" of the nations, personal "adversaries," and demons of negative natural processes. All these categories have positive angelic counterparts: Origen speaks of good angels of the nations, good guardian angels, and good angels of nature; and he regards these as the only divine agents with full legitimacy. It is important to note that Origen sometimes says that good angels discipline (or even punish) sinners on God's behalf, but this theme is less central to Origen's theodicy than punishment through demons, and it will feature minimally in our study.

3.3 Punishment and Divine Wrath

To understand the role avenging demonic agents play in Origen's theodicy, we must briefly review what sort of divine punishment he considered worthy of God. Unlike Marcion, Origen believed in divine punishment and held that it involved true and profound suffering. But, as we have seen in Sections 1.5, 1.5.2, and 1.5.4, Origen qualified this claim in two ways. First, he typically (but not always) emphasizes that God does not directly punish people. God's worst punishment is not to punish at all.[365] And, when he does punish, this often means that he simply lets people experience the natural consequences of their sins. Origen often returns to Isaiah 50.11: You must "walk" in the "fire you have kindled."[366] Part of the suffering caused by the fire sinners light under themselves is the disgust with sin that indulgence eventually brings; but it also involves subjection to demons. According to Origen, sin creates distance from God's protective, watchful presence (ἐπισκοπή) and forges a painful connection with Satan. When Scripture says that God "hands over" sinners to demonic discipline, it simply means that he allows this natural process to occur. Origen's second

---

[364] *Cels.* 8.31–33 (242–46).
[365] *Hom. Jer.* 50.2.4–5 (SC 238:344–48).
[366] For example, *Hom. Ezech.* 3.7 (SC 352:140–42).

qualification of divine punishment is that it is always a benevolent effort to heal the sickness of sin and save the soul. To uphold this idea, Origen had to show that Scriptural references to God's "wrath" do not indicate a vindictive desire to make victims suffer. His approach to this problem was part of his larger engagement with Scriptural anthropomorphism, and it is to this that we now turn.

Many passages in Scripture can be taken to indicate the corporeality of God; and Stoicism supported the idea that the divine is some kind of rarified material.[367] Origen observed that Jews and many Christians thought of God as a man or somehow corporeal,[368] and they included not only "simple and naive" Christians,[369] but even members of the clergy.[370] But these ideas were mocked (*despiciunt*), Origen says, by "philosophers" (primarily Platonists) who "wear out our people," arguing that the "invisible and incorporeal God" cannot "speak" with a literal mouth or "experience human moods."[371] Celsus is an example of one of these mocking philosophers, for he "disparages" Biblical passages in which God appears to have body parts and human passions (ἀνθρωποπαθοῦς).[372] We see here an association between the flux of bodily existence and the passions (πάθη), which Trigg translates "emotional reactions." Passions such as fear, sadness, anger, and ambition were seen as the enemy of virtue because they subject the intellect to change and irrational impulses. Thus, God must be free of passions. Celsus particularly deplored Biblical references to God's "hatred," "anger," and "threats" to "destroy" sinners.[373] Marcionites (and perhaps some Gnostics) objected to the same Old Testament passages, including those in which God is said to be "jealous" or to "do evil."[374]

On the one hand, Origen agreed with Platonists, Marcionites, and Gnostics – God is incorporeal,[375] incorruptible, and unchanging, with no needs (ἀπροσδεής) or negative passions such as "regret" and "wrath,"

---

[367] For Origen's objections, see *Cels.* 1.21 (SC 132:128); *Cels.* 4.13 (SC 136:212–14); *Cels.* 6.70–71 (SC 147:352–60); *Cels.* 8.49 (SC 150:282); *Princ.* 1.1.1 (Behr, 24); *Comm. Jo.* 13.123–50 (SC 222:94–112); Simonetti, "Dio," 119.
[368] *Hom. Gen.* 3.1 (SC 7:114).
[369] *Cels.* 7.27 (SC 150:74).
[370] *Sel. Gen.* D 11 (Metzler, 158–60); compare *Dial.* 12 (SC 67:80); Simonetti, "Dio," 119; Griffin and Paulsen, "Augustine," 101–3.
[371] *Hom. Gen.* 3.1 (SC 7:114).
[372] *Cels.* 4.71 (SC 136:358); Stroumsa, "Incorporeality," 348.
[373] *Cels.* 4.71 (SC 136:358–60); *Cels.* 4.99 (SC 136:432); *Cels.* 6.58 (SC 147:322–24).
[374] *Princ.* 4.2.1 (Behr, 486).
[375] For Origen, this is indicated by the Scriptural term "invisible" (ἀόρατος) (re: Col 1.15 and 1 Tim 1.17).

which are faults even in humans.³⁷⁶ On the other hand, Origen did not think that Scriptural references to these things were grounds for rejection. Still, they required proper interpretation. The word "wrath" posed a special problem for Origen, for "How can the emotion of wrath educate (παιδεύειν)?"³⁷⁷ It seemed to imply hatred, which would confirm the Marcionite belief that even just punishments are "brought to bear against [the wicked] with some degree of hatred" – something inconsistent with the goodness of God.³⁷⁸

To explain why Scripture refers to God's body parts and emotions, Origen pointed to Deuteronomy 8.5 and 1.31: "The Lord your God has taught you (ἐπαίδευσε) as a man would teach his son," and, "he has born [the human] disposition (τροποφορεῖν), as a man [bears the disposition] of his son."³⁷⁹ For Origen, this means that God is like an adult who adapts his language when speaking to children, using simple, childlike words and concepts.³⁸⁰ Scripture condescends to our level when it refers to God's "hand" and "foot," but this does not mean that God is at our level. These words are analogies for his incorporeal "powers."³⁸¹ The same is true of references to God's physical actions and emotions, such as sleeping, repenting, threatening, and being angry. But Origen explains these not just as analogies but also as a kind of divine pretending that is pedagogically useful "for the many."³⁸² When God threatens and uses words such as "if," he pretends³⁸³ that he does not know whether people will choose good or evil, because this promotes repentance.³⁸⁴ To inspire fruitful fear, God speaks of having emotions such as "wrath," but these dramatized speeches (προσωποποιοῦντος θεοῦ) are not fitting to his true nature (ἁρμοζόντως ἑαυτῷ).³⁸⁵ Similarly, good parents hide the kindness they feel and "make a frightening face" in order to save their children from vices.³⁸⁶

---

³⁷⁶ *Princ.* Pref. 8–9 (Behr, 18–20); *Hom. Jer.* 18.6.2 (SC 238:196); *Cels.* 4.72 (SC 136:360–64); *Hom. Ps. 77*, 7.7 (GCS 19NS:446–48); re: Ps 36.8 and Col 3.8. On the passion of wrath, see Solheid, *Pedagogy*, 78–80. See also Koch, *Pronoia*, 21.
³⁷⁷ *Cels.* 4.72 (SC 136:364).
³⁷⁸ *Princ.* 2.5.1–3 (Behr, 190).
³⁷⁹ *Hom. Jer.* 18.6.3 (SC 238:196–98).
³⁸⁰ *Hom. Jer.* 18.6.4–5 (SC 238:198–202).
³⁸¹ *Princ.* 2.8.5 (Behr, 232–34); Simonetti, "Dio," 119–20.
³⁸² *Cels.* 4.71 (SC 136:358–60).
³⁸³ Origen uses ὑποκρίνομαι and προσποιέομαι.
³⁸⁴ *Hom. Jer.* 18.6.5 (SC 238:200–2).
³⁸⁵ *Cels.* 4.71 (SC 136:360).
³⁸⁶ *Hom. Jer.* 18.6.7 (SC 238:202).

This might explain the *threat* of wrath, but what about the *experience* of wrath as suffering imposed by God? Of course, this suffering is remedial,[387] and "truly [God] is neither wrathful nor angry, but you will suffer the [typical manifestations] of wrath and of anger, when you come upon unendurable hardships due to [your] evil. It is then that you are taught (παιδεύσῃ) by what is called the wrath of God."[388] But what is "called the wrath of God"? One predictable answer is that it is the self-punishment of sinners who are "storing up wrath" for themselves (re: Rom 2.5).[389] But the other answer, as we will see, is that "wrath" refers to the punishing demons who afflict sinners. God may "send" them out, or he may "hand over" or "abandon" sinners to them; but, he himself does not strike the blow.

So far, this section has (1) reviewed Origen's belief that even evil demons have useful roles in God's providential arrangement of the world and that one of these roles is the punishment of sinners; (2) outlined the three categories of demons that play this role; and (3) shown that Origen tries to distance God from vindictive punishment and from the direct affliction of sinners and indicated how demons function in this theodicy. We are now ready to examine in detail the network of Biblical passages that support Origen's beliefs about punishing demons and to consider their theological function.

3.4 God's Executioners (Psalm 78.49)

As noted in Section 2, Exodus 12.23 indicates that God killed the firstborn of the sinful Egyptians by the agency of "the Destroyer"; and Psalm 78.49–50 (= Ps 77 in LXX) says that he accomplished the last plague when "He let loose on them his fierce anger, wrath, indignation, and distress, a company of destroying angels." In the Septuagint, this is translated: "He sent out (ἐξαπέστειλεν) against them the wrath of his anger, anger and wrath and affliction – a dispatch through evil angels" (ἀποστολὴν δι' ἀγγέλων πονηρῶν). This appears to have been a key passage in Origen's reflection, though it is connected to his exegesis of many other passages and themes. In the following text, we will consider relevant sections of Origen's writings, most of which date from his late Caesarean period, between the mid 240s and 249.

---

[387] *Cels.* 4.72 (SC 136:362).
[388] *Hom. Jer.* 18.6.7 (SC 238:204).
[389] *Cels.* 4.73 (SC 136:364–66).

Origen's *Commentary on Romans*, dating from the mid 240s,[390] exists primarily in Rufinus' Latin translation (c. 406/7), which abbreviated the original by fifty percent and may contain alterations. Still, it is an invaluable resource. In Book 1.19, Rufinus' Origen (hereafter "Origen") examines Romans 1.18–19, where Paul writes that God's wrath is being "revealed from heaven" against wicked humans. This leads Origen to a general discussion of divine wrath in Scripture and the proper interpretation of it.[391] One of his main observations is that, in Scripture, divine wrath "seems sometimes" to refer to "the power (*uirtus ipsa*) that is in charge of the ministers of punishments and inflicts penalties upon sinners" (*quae praeest poenarum ministris et quae supplicia infert peccatoribus*). Origen supports this with a cryptic reference to the story of David's census in 2 Samuel 24.1 (which we will examine in Section 3.6), but his main argument rests on Psalm 78.49: "He dispatched against them the wrath of his rage, tribulation and wrath through evil angels."[392] For Origen, this shows that divine punishments are enacted by evil angelic ministers who receive their authority (*potestatem*) "from heaven."[393]

Later in his *Commentary on Romans*, Origen returns to this topic. His discussion of Romans 8.14–15 leads him to the observation that the word "spirit" in Scripture can refer to "various spirits."[394] After a discussion of the Holy Spirit and angelic spirits,[395] he progresses to cases where "spirit" refers to "evil" spirits and angels. Origen's first example is Psalm 78.49: "He sent out against them the wrath of his indignation, a dispatch through evil angels." He follows this with references to the malevolent spirits (*spiritus malignus*) God sent to torment Saul (1 Sam 16.14) and to divide Abimelech and the men of Shechem (Judg 9.23). Origen concludes:

> This malevolent spirit (*spiritus malignus*), which went out either to strangle Saul or to divide Ambimelech and the Shechemites, is reported both *to have gone out* and *to have been sent* by the Lord (*a Domino*). Thus, it must certainly be understood to have been sent as a sort of executioner (*tamquam carnifex*) to exact penalties from sinners (*ad exigendas de peccatoribus poenas*). And although [these spirits] are called "evil" on account of their own purpose and will (*propter propositum suum voluntatemque*), nevertheless among those who deserve punishment, they provide a service to the divine will (*divinae voluntati exhibent ministerium*).[396]

---

[390] Nautin, *Origène*, 386, 411; Scheck, *Origen*, 8–9n28.
[391] *Comm. Rom.* 1.19.1 (SC 532:236–38).
[392] *Comm. Rom.* 1.19.3 (SC 532:238–40).
[393] *Comm. Rom.* 1.19.4 (SC 532:240).
[394] *Comm. Rom.* 7.1.1 (SC 543:242).
[395] *Comm. Rom.* 7.1.2 (SC 543:244–46).
[396] *Comm. Rom.* 7.1.3 (SC 543:246–48).

As an example of this kind of service, Origen cites 1 Kings 22.19–23, where God commissions an evil spirit to lie to the prophets of Ahab and entice him to go to war, where he will die.[397] This was an important passage for Origen. In *First Principles*, he observes: "This passage clearly shows that a certain spirit chose by its own will and purpose (*voluntate et proposito suo*) to mislead and enact deception; but God takes advantage of [(or "makes use of")] this spirit (*quo spiritu abutitur*) to slaughter Ahab, who deserved to suffer."[398]

Another reference to Psalm 78.49, along with demonic "executioners" (Gk: δήμιοι), appears in *Against Celsus* (AD 248–249),[399] whose special polemical context will be considered later. Origen says that "one needs very profound knowledge" to establish whether wicked demons (μοχθηροὶ δαίμονες) are "like bandits" who set up their own rebel "confederacies" or whether they are ever "like executioners (ὡς δήμιοι) in cities and those appointed for severe but necessary tasks in states." In the latter case, they would be "appointed (τεταγμένοι) to certain [tasks] by God's Logos, as he administers the universe."[400] In Book 8.31–33, Origen returns to this theme. He ventures to say that demons, who do nothing good, bring about famines, droughts, and polluted air that damages agriculture and causes plague. And yet, in God's plan, these attacks serve to "turn people back" from evil or "to train (εἰς γυμνάσιον) rational beings." In this process, people's hidden dispositions are revealed, whether good or bad. In fact, demons function like God's executioners (δήμιοι): they are the direct agents (αὐτουργοῦσι) of all the bad things they do; but they act with authority they have received by some kind of divine decision (κρίσει τινὶ θείᾳ λαβόντες ἐξουσίαν).[401]

Origen's Scriptural support for this perspective is Psalm 78.49: "Now, the psalmist bears witness to the fact that certain wicked angels are the proximate agents (αὐτουργεῖται) of such severe disasters (τὰ σκυθρωπότερα) but that they act by divine appointment (θείᾳ κρίσει) when he says: 'He sent out against them the wrath of his anger, anger and wrath and affliction, a dispatch through wicked angels.'"[402] As we noted earlier, the topic of Psalm 78.49 is the last plague upon Egypt. This is particularly fitting, since Origen has just mentioned the droughts and plagues caused by demons. In Origen's *Homilies on Ezekiel*, he explicitly connects the evil angels of Psalm

---

[397] *Comm. Rom.* 7.1.3 (SC 543:248).
[398] *Princ.* 3.2.1 (Behr, 380–82).
[399] Nautin, *Origène*, 375–76, 381, 412; Chadwick, *Origen*, xiv–xv.
[400] *Cels.* 7.70 (SC 150:176).
[401] *Cels.* 8.31 (SC 150:242).
[402] *Cels.* 8.32 (SC 150:242).

78.49 and the Destroyer of the firstborn in Exodus.[403] This is consistent with the idea that the destroying angel (ὀλεθρευτὴς) of Exodus was the devil, which Origen considers in *First Principles* and affirms in *Against Celsus*.[404] In another interpretive paradigm, however, Origen emphasizes the Destroyer's role in saving the Israelites from Egypt; and he can even be understood figuratively as an image of Christ who destroys the firstborn of demonic power through his own Passover.[405]

Origen's recently discovered *Homilies on the Psalms* were delivered just after *Against Celsus*, so perhaps in 249.[406] *Homilies on Psalm 77*, 7.7[407] is important for our study, for here Psalm 78.49 (= Ps 77 in LXX) is the focus of exegesis. Significantly, the topic is God's wrath, as it is in *Commentary on Romans* 1.19. Origen seems to have Marcion and Valentinus in mind when he speaks of those who think that God's wrath is a passion (πάθος).[408] His first observation about Psalm 78.49 is that God's "wrath" is something that is "sent out" (ἐξαποστέλεται).[409] Origen's conclusion is that this "wrath" must be "different than the one whose wrath it is," and that in fact it may be a living being (ζῷον). Origen appears to be referring to the "wicked angels" mentioned in the passage. In support of this idea, Origen cites Paul's comment in Ephesians 2.3 that "we were children of wrath by nature." Although Origen does not make his argument explicit, he appears to be referring to the fact that, earlier in Ephesians 2, the state of being "children of wrath" is equated with "having walked ... according to the ruler of the authority over the air, the spirit now active in the sons of disobedience" (Eph 2.2). Thus, Ephesians 2.2–3 associates the experience of "wrath" with being under the influence of the devil. The fact that this is Origen's point is made surer by a passage in the *Commentary on John* where Origen associates being children of wrath in Ephesians 2.3 with Jesus' comments about people being children of the devil in John 8.44.[410] Going back to *Homilies on Psalm 77*, 7.7, Origen concludes, God sends his wrath "through wicked angels" "for those who deserve such things."

As further support for this idea, Origen turns to 1 Corinthians 5.4–5, where Paul orders the Corinthian sinner to be handed over to Satan for

---

[403] *Hom. Ezech.* 5.2.2 (SC 352:196).
[404] *Princ.* 3.2.1 (Behr, 380); *Cels.* 6.43 (SC 147:284).
[405] *Hom. Num.* 3.4.2 (SC 415:90–92).
[406] Perrone, "Dating," 247–49.
[407] *Hom. Ps. 77*, 7.7 (GCS 19NS:446–48). See similar comments in *Hom. Ps. 77*, 5.3 (GCS 19NS:410–12).
[408] Compare Perrone, "Scrittura," 178.
[409] For discussion, see Solheid, *Pedagogy*, 78–80.
[410] *Comm. Jo.* 20.217–19 (SC 290:262–64).

discipline; but we will consider this in Section 3.5. To sum up the present discussion of Origen's exegesis of Psalm 78.49: Origen shows concern that references to divine wrath in Scripture be properly understood – particularly that they not be taken to indicated that God has the emotional reaction (πάθος) of anger. The Psalm's reference to "sending out" wrath and its apparent identification of God's "wrath" with "a dispatch of wicked angels" are important, for they show that God's wrath is not a πάθος or something within God. When wrath is experienced, wicked demons are those who directly inflict it; God (or his Logos) merely appoints them for this task. Their own will is evil, but they offer a service to God, so they can be called his "executioners."

3.5 "Deliver This Man to Satan" (1 Cor 5.5; 1 Tim 1.20)

As just noted, in *Homilies on Psalm 77*, 7.7, Origen cites 1 Corinthians 5.5 in support of his claim that Scriptural references to God's "wrath" refer to the pain inflicted by evil angels. Although Paul made no mention of "wrath," Origen believes this passage shows that the Apostle, like God, "sent forth" wrath upon "the sexual sinner at Corinth" when he "handed him over" "to Satan for the destruction of his flesh."[411]

In 1 Corinthians 5.5, the purpose of this is "in order that his spirit may be saved in the day of the Lord." Similarly, when the author of 1 Timothy 1.20 says that he has "handed over (παρέδωκα) [Hymenaeus and Alexander] to Satan," the intent is that "they may be taught (παιδευθῶσιν) not to blaspheme." Not surprisingly, Origen often uses these passages to show that God's punishments are intended for people's good. *Homilies on Psalm 77*, 7.7, is no exception, for Origen concludes that God's dispatch of wrath is in keeping with his arguments in favor of "a good God." Many people who "are not willing to pay attention to the Logos" are only "forced to turn and seek again for God" "when wicked spirits come." Thus, God's "calling [of people] often happens through wicked angels."[412] In several other passages, Origen uses 1 Cor 5.5 to show that when God "kills" or imposes "death" it is a death to sin that brings life and salvation to the soul.[413] Paul's handing over of sinners to Satan is one of the harsh but necessary remedies of the divine Physician.[414]

---

[411] *Hom. Ps. 77*, 7.7 (GCS 19NS:446).
[412] *Hom. Ps. 77*, 7.7 (GCS 19NS:446–47).
[413] *Comm. Rom.* 6.6.6 (SC 543:132); *Comm. Rom.* 6.13.5 (SC 543:220–22); *Hom. Lev.* 3.4.3–5 (SC 286:138–40); *Hom. Lev.*14.4.6 (SC 287:248).
[414] *Philoc.* 27.8 (SC 226:296).

For Origen, Old Testament enemies were inspired by, and/or are figures of, Satan. Thus, there is a parallel between the sinful Israelites who were handed over to the Assyrians and sinful Christians who are handed over to Satan (re: 1 Tim 1.20).[415] Just as God repeatedly warned the Israelites before abandoning them to captivity under Nebuchadnezzar, so he repeatedly warns Christians before he hands them over to the spiritual Nebuchadnezzar (Satan) and the spiritual Babylonians (οἱ νοητοὶ Βαβυλώνιοι = demons) who will tear them in pieces (σπαράξωσιν).[416] But God's goal is not to annihilate the sinner, for "Assyrians" (according to Origen's etymology) means "those who direct," indicating that slavery to Satan will serve to correct and restore.[417]

In addition, Origen argues that God does not, in fact, actively "hand over" people to Satan: he simply withdraws from sinners and lets demons seize the "empty house" (re: Matt 12.43–45). Thus, God does not impose wrath; sinners store it up for themselves (re: Rom 2.5). Because being consigned to Satan is the natural corollary of sin, neither God, nor the Apostle Paul, can be accused of doing anything harsh.[418]

For Origen and his community, as well as for Paul, handing serious sinners over to Satan included removing them from the Church.[419] According to Origen, although this should be a last resort and must be performed in love,[420] it cannot be omitted in the case of grievous sin.[421] If people hide their sin from ecclesiastical leaders, God still sees it and hands them over to Satan himself.[422] Origen says that the torments of false Christians under Satan are worse than those of pagans. They suffer the "destruction of the flesh" (re: 1 Cor 5.5), which seems to include bodily suffering; but they may also suffer public shame. If penitents spend the allotted time of their exclusion from the Church embracing suffering under the enemy and practicing virtue, they will receive the fruit of salvation. If they do not, they will suffer eternally (re: Luke 16.25).[423]

---

[415] *Hom. Num.* 19.4.2–4 (SC 442:364–68).
[416] *Hom. Jer.* 1.3.2–1.4.2 (SC 232:198–202); *Fr. Jer.* 48.125 (GCS 6:222).
[417] *Hom. Num.* 19.3.3 (SC 442:362).
[418] *Hom. Gen.* 16.2 (SC 7:376); compare *Hom. Ezech.* 3.8.5–4 (SC 352:146–48).
[419] Rahner, "La doctrine," 255, 264–66.
[420] *Comm. Matt.* 16.8 (GCS 40:496).
[421] *Hom. Jes. Nav.* 7.6 (SC 71:208–10).
[422] *Fr. Jer.* 48.125 (GCS 6:222).
[423] *Hom. Lev.* 3.4.4–5 (SC 286:140–42); *Hom. Lev.* 14.4.6 (SC 287:246–48); *Fr. Jer.* 48.125 (GCS 6:222); *Hom. Ezech.* 12.3 (SC 352:388–92).

More importantly for the present project, the question of divine wrath reappears in connection with 1 Corinthians 5.5 in *Scholia on Revelation* 30.[424] Here, Origen says that Scriptural references to human emotions, as well as to body parts, are analogical when applied to God. When Scripture speaks of "God's wrath," people should not think that he has an emotional reaction (πάθος), any more than they should think that he has ears. *Human anger is something within humans, but God's* "anger" is something "outside of" him. Origen implies that the external nature of divine wrath makes it appropriate for those who have distanced themselves from God – they, too, are outside of him. And what is this external divine wrath to which people are said to be "handed over" (παραδίδονται) in Scripture? "The wrath of God," Origen says, "is the devil."[425] For support, Origen turns to a detailed treatment of the two versions of the story of David's census, which we will consider in Section 3.6.[426] At the end of this discussion, he returns to the concept that God's anger is "sent out."[427] Anything "sent out" must be distinct from the person who sends it. So, Origen concludes, when people are said to be "handed over to the wrath of God," "it must be understood that they are handed over to the devil, as Paul handed over (παρέδωκε) the Corinthian, or those he handed over to Satan to be taught not to blaspheme."[428]

We have seen that the references to pedagogy and saving the soul in 1 Corinthians 5.5 and 1 Timothy 1.20 support Origen's claim that God punishes only to heal and restore. In addition, Origen notes that the concept of "handing over" distances God from sinners and their punishment, just as the concept of "sending out" in Psalm 78.49. But, in fact, even the concept of "handing over" is too active for Origen, and he says that, in reality, God simply withdraws from sinners and lets them experience the natural bondage to Satan their actions have produced. Although the word "wrath" does not appear in 1 Corinthians 5.5 or 1 Timothy 1.20, Origen uses the "handing over" paradigm, as well as the "sending out" paradigm to identify God's wrath as something external to himself, which is, in fact,

---

[424] The scholarly consensus that attributed these scholia to Origen has been challenged, but not successfully, by Tzamalikos, *Ancient Commentary*, 91–94. For critique, see Alciati, "Il Cassiano"; Allen, "Reception," 141–43.

[425] καί ἐστιν ὀργὴ θεοῦ ὁ διάβολος. Tzamalikos (*Ancient Commentary*, 159n5) points to a similar perspective in Didymus the Blind, *Commentarii in Psalmos 40–44.4* (Gronewald, 309).

[426] According to Tzamalikos (*Ancient Commentary*, 159n20), Origen was the first to use 2 Sam 24.1 and 1 Chron 21.1 to argue that God's wrath refers to the devil.

[427] Re: Exod 15.7 and possibly re: Ps 78.49 (= Ps 77 in LXX).

[428] *Schol. Apoc.* 30.268r–69v (Tzamalikos, 159–60), re: 1 Cor 5.5 and 1 Tim 1.20.

Satan and his angels. Origen obviously regarded Psalm 78.49 as critical evidence for this thesis, but he also depended on the two versions of the story of David's census, to which we now turn.

3.6 Satan and the Census (2 Sam 24; 1 Chron 21)

At least three extant passages in Origen cite the story of David's census as evidence that God's wrath is the devil. In *Commentary on Romans* 1.19.3,[429] of which we have already considered other aspects, Origen cites the reference to the Lord's wrath inciting David to sin (2 Sam 24.1) to support his claim that God's "wrath" sometimes refers to Satan in his role as the punisher of sinners. Origen's point, although not explicit, seems to be that God's "wrath" in 2 Samuel 24.1 is playing the same role as "Satan" in 1 Chronicles 21.1 – both are said to have incited David's sin. Thus, divine "wrath" refers to Satan's activity.

This argument is easier to discern in *Against Celsus* 4.71–73.[430] Here, Origen argues that God's wrath is not a passion (πάθος) because the passion of wrath is a fault (even in humans) and inspires vindictive (not pedagogical) punishments. Some Scripture passages use the word "wrath" because it makes sense to simple people and inspires them to repent, but it is not in keeping with God's true nature (ἁρμοζόντως ἑαυτῷ). The "very skillful" will understand other passages that speak more spiritually; and these show, Origen implies, how to interpret references to wrath figuratively (τροπολογεῖσθαι) (re: 1 Cor 2.13). His first point is that some passages identify the purpose of God's anger as correction (παιδεύω) (re: Ps 6.1 and Jer 10.24), and this guides one to interpret other references to "wrath" as corrective (non-vindictive). Second, Origen cites 2 Samuel 24.1, where "the wrath of God persuaded (ἀναπείθουσαν) David to number the people," and 1 Chronicles 21.1, where "the devil does so." According to Origen, "Anyone who reads these accounts and examines their statements in conjunction will see for what [purpose] the wrath is appointed."[431]

But how so? The main difference between the passages, and the one Origen highlights, is that one says God's wrath enticed David to sin, and the other says that "the devil" did so (in the LXX, "satan"). The gem that Origen thinks is apparent to the discerning reader is that God's "wrath" in 2 Samuel 24.1 is a figurative expression for "the devil" in 1 Chronicles 21.1.

---

[429] SC 532:238.
[430] SC 136:358–66.
[431] Ἀναγνοὺς ... καὶ συνεξετάζων ἀλλήλοις τὰ ῥητὰ ὄψεται ἐπὶ τίνος τάσσεται ἡ ὀργή.

The devil seems to be one of the "more severe directives" (σκυθρωποτέρων ἀγωγῶν) God employs to educate and discipline sinners. This is what was implied in *Commentary on Romans* 1.19.3. What strengthens the interpretation in *Against Celsus* 4.71–73 is that Origen identifies the "wrath" that incited David to the census as the same "wrath" "of which [converts] were all children" in Ephesians 2.3 – a wrath that Ephesians associates with bondage to the devil. As we saw, Origen cited this same passage in *Homilies on Psalm 77*, 7.7, to make a similar point.

All of this is crystal clear in Origen's exegesis of the census stories in *Scholia on Revelation* 30.[432] Origen notes that 2 Samuel 24.1 says, "The wrath of the Lord ... incited David," but 1 Chronicles 21.1 says, "the devil ... incited David," indicating that God's wrath is in fact the devil. But Origen has two more points. First, in 2 Samuel 24.1, the participle "saying" (λέγων), which introduces the command to sin by numbering the people, should agree with the grammatically feminine subject "wrath" (ὀργή), but instead it is grammatically masculine. Thus, the "wrath" that incited David to sin has become something masculine, which Origen takes as support for his belief that "wrath" is an analogy for the devil.

Origen's final point in this passage is that our interpretation of 2 Samuel 24.1 ("The wrath of the Lord ... incited David") must be guided by the knowledge that God does not incite people to sin. This would be particularly unjust in the census story, since God goes on to punish people for the sin he supposedly incited. It is normal, on the other hand, for the devil to persuade people to sin; and God is fully justified in punishing those who succumb to these persuasions. So, Origen concludes, both 2 Samuel and 1 Chronicles refer to the devil as the incitement to sin,[433] but one uses the common expression "devil," while the other, by calling him "wrath of the Lord," uses an expression "hidden from the majority."[434] Origen notes that the same phrase ("wrath of the Lord" – ὀργὴν Κυρίου) is used analogically to refer to the devil in the Song of Moses: "You sent out your wrath and it consumed [the Egyptians] as stubble" (re: Exod 15.7).

3.7 The Wrath-As-Devil Hermeneutic

We have seen how the two versions of the census story, along with Psalm 78.49, support Origen's claim that God's "wrath" refers to the devil; but, we have also seen Origen exhort "very skillful" readers to use these more

---

[432] *Schol. Apoc.* 30.268r–69r (Tzamalikos, 159–60).
[433] διάβολος δ' ἀμφοτέρων τῶν προσηγοριῶν ὠνομάσθη.
[434] τῆς τοὺς πολλοὺς λανθανούσης.

spiritual passages to interpret other references to God's wrath. In fact, we have seen him do it. For Origen, the wrath God "sent out" in Exodus 15.7 (just mentioned previously) must be the devil, and this may serve to distance God from having directly "consumed [the Egyptians] as stubble." We might put in the same category Origen's interpretation of 2 Samuel's version of the census story, where the identification of God's "wrath" as Satan serves to absolve God from having incited David's sin.

Another interesting example of this hermeneutical principle is Origen's interpretation of Numbers 16.43–50. When the Israelites murmured against Moses after the punishment of Korah, the text says that wrath went out from God, who intended to destroy the people with a plague (Num 16.44–50). But Origen says that *"a certain power (virtutem) was sent by God to devastate the people with death,"* and he identifies this power as the "devastating angel" (*angelum vastantem*). Origen notes that Aaron the priest stood between the dead and the living with a censor and stopped the plague, having shamed (*erubuisse*) the Devastator, who was terrified (*expavit*). This was because the angel recognized in Aaron the figure of Christ, the High Priest, who would come with the censor of his flesh and "destroy him who held the power of death, who is the devil" (re: Heb 2.14).[435]

Without even acknowledging the switch, Origen has interpreted the divine "wrath" in this passage as the devil; but, based on what we have seen, this makes perfect sense. Surely the reference to "wrath" having "gone out" from God and causing a plague in Numbers 16 made Origen think of Psalm 78.49, in which the "wrath" God "sent" to destroy the firstborn of Egypt (possibly through a plague) is identified as a group of evil angels. Based on this Psalm, it was natural (as we have seen) for Origen to identify *the* Destroyer of the firstborn in Exodus 12.3 as the devil. Thus, the plague-producing wrath of God in Numbers 16 had to be the devil or the "Devastator." And, of course, we can see theodicy throughout: God directs the destruction of the Egyptian firstborn and of the rebellious Israelites, but he himself is not a slaughterer.

We must remember that Origen often inherited and built on earlier readings. Paul's reference to those who "grumbled" and "were destroyed by the Destroyer" (1 Cor 10.10) is probably a reference to Numbers 16.41–49. If so, he or the tradition he drew from had already interpreted God's plague-causing wrath in Numbers 16 as the destroying angel of Exodus 12.23. To take a step further, some scholars think that the

---

[435] *Hom. Num.* 9.5.1–3 (SC 415:242–44).

"Destroyer" in 1 Corinthians 10.10 and Hebrews 11.28 is a reference to Satan.[436] Origen may have been treading in a well-worn path.

3.8 Demons as Creditors and Tax-Collectors

So far, we have examined two paradigms: one in which God's wrath refers to demons who are "sent out" as the "executioners" of sinners and the other in which God "hands over" sinners to Satan for punishment. We now turn to a third paradigm in which demons function as God's creditors or "tax collectors."

As Origen says, he "frequently and in many cases" claims that "sin is a debt" (Lt *debitum*; Gk ὀφείλημα).[437] He points out that Jesus calls sin a debt, both in the *Pater noster* (τὰ ὀφειλήματα – re: Matt 6.12) and in his discussion with Simon the Pharisee about the sinful woman (ὀφείλω – re: Luke 7.37–48).[438] Origen also notes the sinner's "record of debt" in Colossians 2.14.[439] In the ancient world, people could be enslaved because of their debts,[440] so Origen associates the debt of sin with New Testament references to the slavery of sin.[441] According to him, people were "sold" into slavery for their sins and had to be "bought back" or "ransomed" by Jesus.[442]

In one confusing paradigm, Origen speaks of the "debt," not as something that sinners owe, but as something that is owed to them, in repayment for their sin. According to Origen, righteousness never earns anything from God, who gives gifts and not wages;[443] but the works of iniquity *do* earn something;[444] and "the debt that is paid back" for them is "the retribution of punishment," for the "wages of sin is death" (re: Rom 6.23).[445] Thus, *someone* is obligated to pay to sinners the punishment and death they have earned, but it is not God; it is, as we will see, the devil.

---

[436] Stokes, *The Satan*, 196n6; Farrar and Williams, "Diabolical Data," 54–56.
[437] *Comm. Rom.* 9.30.4 (SC 555:182). For other passages in which he calls sin a debt, see *Hom. Luc.* 35.10–13 (SC 87:424–28); *Hom. Jer.* 14.4 (SC 238:70–72).
[438] *Comm. Rom.* 4.1.13 (SC 539:194); *Or.* 28.1 (GCS 3:375–76).
[439] *Comm. Rom.* 5.3.2 (SC 539:422); *Comm. Rom.* 5.9.7 (SC 539:492); *Hom. Jer.* 15.5.1 (SC 238:122); *Or* 28.5 (GCS 3:378); *Hom. Gen.* 13.4 (SC 7:330).
[440] *Hom. Luc.* 23.6 (SC 87:318–20).
[441] *Comm. Rom.* 5.3.2 (SC 539:422); *Hom. Luc.* 23.6 (SC 87:318–20); *Fr. Eph.* 3 (Gregg, 237). Origen cites passages such as John 8.34; Rom 6.16–20, 8.15; 2 Pet 2.19; and Heb 2.15.
[442] *Hom. Exod.* 6.9 (SC 321:192–96); *Comm. Rom.* 2.9.34 (SC 532:410); *Comm. Matt.* 16.8 (GCS 40:498–99). Origen cites passages such as Matt 20.28; Mark 10.45; Acts 20.28; 1 Cor. 6:20; Gal 3.13; 1 Pet 1.18–19; and Rev 5.9.
[443] Re: John 3.34 and Rom 4.4.
[444] Re: Matt 7.23/Luke 13.27.
[445] *Comm. Rom.* 4.1.14–15 (SC 539:196).

This idea that sinners have "earned" punishment and death emphasizes that these things are self-imposed – a theme that appears regularly in Origen's more common paradigm, in which sinners "owe" a debt of punishment and death (as opposed to it being owed *to them*). Noting that the word used for the sinner's "record of debt" in Colossians 2.14 (Gk χειρόγραφον; Lt *chirographum*) indicates something written (γραφον) with one's own hand (χείρ), Origen claims that God does not write this document: people sign away their own freedom and life in "the handwriting of sin."[446] Sometimes Origen expresses this by comparing sin to money. When people sin, they receive this money and so enter into debt. Records of the debt of sin (*peccati chirographa*) are written, as well as documents of servitude (*tabulas servitutis*).[447] And the debt sin obligates one to pay is, as we have seen earlier, suffering and death. People sign away their own immortality. In his exegesis of Psalm 22.15 (= Ps 21.16 in LXX), Origen says that God does not subject the soul to death; it subjects itself.[448]

Thus, God does not write people's "record of debt"; but Origen also claims that God is not the one to whom the debt is owed. The *chirographum* ("IOU" in Thomas Scheck's translation of the *Commentary on Romans*)[449] is handed over to "death," not to God.[450] In this passage, Origen treats "death" as accompanied by, or associated with, or a symbol of, the devil, who "holds the power of death" (re: Heb 2.14).[451] Elsewhere he says explicitly that sinners were "sold for [their] sins" to the devil. "What sort of thing did the devil give to purchase [them]?" He bought them by giving them sin, which is "the money of the devil" (*pecunia diaboli*).[452] According to Origen,

> Theft, false testimony, rapaciousness, violence, all these are the revenue[453] (*census*) and the treasure of the devil; for money (*pecunia*) of this sort comes from his mint. Therefore, with this sin he buys those he buys, and he makes into his slaves all those who have accepted any of this sort of revenue (*censu*).[454]

---

[446] *Hom. Gen.* 13.4 (SC 7:330).
[447] *Hom. Exod.* 6.9 (SC 321:192–96).
[448] *Comm. Rom.* 5.3.2 (SC 539:422).
[449] Scheck, *Origen*, 336.
[450] *Comm. Rom.* 5.3.2 (SC 539:422).
[451] *Comm. Rom.* 5.3.5–6 (SC 539:426–28).
[452] *Hom. Exod.* 6.9 (SC 321:192).
[453] Following Borret's translation of *census* as *revenu* (SC 321:195).
[454] *Hom. Exod.* 6.9 (SC 321:194).

Just as Jesus pointed out that Roman coins with the image of the emperor had to be paid to the emperor (re: Matt 22.20), so "on [the coin of] sin is the image and inscription of the devil," and those who receive it must pay the devil back for his property.[455]

As we will see shortly, it is Christ who initially pays this debt at conversion and baptism; but what can Christians do who sin and slip back into debt and slavery to the devil? They can get free "by repenting, weeping, and making satisfaction."[456] Here we see a recurring theme, which is that the sinner's debt of death can be paid through the voluntary death of fleshly mortification and penance. The principle is that those who die to sin can once more be alive in Christ (re: Rom 6.11). This brings to mind Origen's exhortation to sinners who have been handed over to Satan (re: 1 Cor 5.5) to endure the "destruction of the flesh," in order to be saved.

Origen's belief that the debt of death and suffering is paid to (or exacted by) the devil and his demons appears in his exegesis of Romans 13.1–7, where Paul says that human "authorities" (ἐξουσίαι) and "rulers" (ἄρχοντες) are God's servants (διάκονος), so people should be subject to them and pay taxes. In this way, Paul says, people will avoid God's wrath, for these rulers are "avengers of wrath" (ἔκδικος εἰς ὀργὴν) against those who do evil. According to Origen, this passage contains "mysteries" (*sacramentis*), for the "authorities" Paul mentions are figures of the evil angels that sinners ought to fear and to whom they must be subject and pay "tax." As Paul indicates, these angels function as God's servants, for "all creatures and spirits ... serve God and provide to him the service for which they have shown themselves suited ... even if they are of depraved and evil intent." Origen includes these evil spirits among the "ministering spirits sent to minister on behalf of those who will receive the inheritance of salvation" in Hebrews 1.14.[457]

These demonic tax collectors may be God's ministers, but the fact that sinners are subject to them is not God's doing but the natural consequence of sin. The worldly disposition of demons makes them suited for the management of worldly things. Thus, when humans choose to be worldly, "it is necessary" that they come under the purview of these "ministers of the world" (re: Rom 8.5, 8.12). And since they are now subjects of demonic rulers, Paul naturally says they owe these rulers taxes

---

[455] Ibid.
[456] Ibid.
[457] *Comm. Rom.* 9.30.1 (SC 555:178).

(re: Rom 13.7).[458] People who are bound up with worldly things have "Caesar's inscription on them" and thus must render to Caesar what is Caesar's (re: Matt 22.20–21). The goal is to be like Peter and John, who had no "gold and silver" (re: Acts 3.6) and thus had "nothing to give back to Caesar."[459] Christ, of course, had "nothing of Caesar's in himself" and so "the ruler (*Princeps*) of this world" found nothing of his own in him (re: Jn 14.30).[460]

But what are the taxes sinners must pay? They are the "taxes of the flesh" (*tributa carnis*), paid to the spirits who exact them from people through "various trials." Of course, this payment of suffering is salvific. To pay the tax is to sell all that one has and buy the pearl of the kingdom of heaven (re: Matt 13.45–46).[461] The idea is that one's attachment to worldly things makes one vulnerable to suffering at the hands of worldly spirits, but, ironically, this suffering serves to detach one from worldly things. Once one has achieved this detachment, one is freed from the slavery to demons that is due to sin. Those who have received "the Spirit who is from God" and not "the spirit of this world" (re: 1 Cor 2.12) and have been "crucified" to the world (re: Gal 6.14) are not subject to these spirits.[462]

In his *Homilies on Luke*, Origen emphasizes that, if one does not pay one's dues in this life, one will pay in the next: departed souls will encounter "certain beings seated at the boundary of the world who, as if they had the job of tax collectors (*publicanorum officio*), search very carefully to find anything in ascending souls that belongs to them." The goal is to be like Jesus, for when "the prince of this age" came like a tax collector (*quasi publicanus*), he found nothing of his own in Jesus (re: John 14.30). Similarly, when the "tax collector" Laben chased after Jacob and searched his tents for anything that belonged to him, Jacob had no fear, for he was a holy man (re: Gen 31.32–37). But, as Paul commands, sinners must return taxes to those to whom they owe them (re: Rom 13.7), and many people "are subject to the great peril" of not being able to pay and of being "dragged off because of [their] debt" and imprisoned.[463]

The phrase "dragged off" is a reference to Luke 12.57–59 (cf. Matt 5.25–26), where Jesus exhorts one to "settle with" one's adversary (ἀντίδικος) "on the way" before one reaches the ruler (ἄρχων), "lest he drag you to the judge, and the judge hand you over to the officer (πράκτωρ), and the officer put

---

[458] *Comm. Rom.* 9.30.2–4 (SC 555:180–82).
[459] *Comm. Rom.* 9.25 (SC 555:164).
[460] *Comm. Rom.* 9.30.3 (SC 555:180–82).
[461] *Comm. Rom.* 9.30.3 (SC 555:182).
[462] *Comm. Rom.* 9.30.1 (SC 555:178).
[463] *Hom. Luc.* 23.5–7 (SC 87:318–20).

you in prison ... till you have paid the very last copper." In Origen's exegesis of this passage in *Homilies on Luke* 35,[464] the "ruler" (Lt *princeps*) is one of the wicked angelic rulers of the nations. The "adversary" (*adversarius*) is one of the "angels of iniquity" that the angelic ruler sends to each person to tempt them to sin and so to subject them to his control. If the ruler and the adversary are successful, they will (presumably on the last day) hand their charges over to "the Judge," who is Christ, and he will hand them over to the "debt collector" (Gk πράκτωρ; Lt *exactor*). Christ is the one who forgives; "but the debt collector is not the lord but one appointed as a superintendent by the Lord to exact debts." Thus, "all of us have our own debt collectors," and they "rule over us when we owe something." The debt we will pay is the "penalty" (*damnum*) incurred "for each of our sins" that the Lord has not previously forgiven. Origen says that we will not get out of prison until we have paid the last penny, which may take "infinite ages." But if during earthly life one has followed Paul's command to "pay back [one's] debts to everyone," including "taxes" (*vectigal*) (re: Rom 13.7), then one can have confidence when the debt collector comes to "demand the return" of what one owes. One can "resist him" and say "with an untroubled mind," "I owe you nothing."

The scriptural support for Origen's belief in demons as creditors and tax collectors is less firm than it is for demonic executioners; and we see more reliance on "spiritual" readings of the text. Two influences are clear: first, the post-exilic Jewish tradition of angelic rulers of the nations who, though evil, are appointed by God to punish the wicked; second, Origen's conviction (derived from multiple sources) that God does not directly impose suffering on people. As in the paradigms of God "sending out" punishing demons or "handing over" sinners to Satan, the idea of demonic creditors and tax collectors serves to distance God from what is inconsistent with his nature. At the same time, these tax collectors function as ministers of God, and the suffering they exact is directed by the benevolent pedagogy of providence.

3.9 Threat of the *Paterfamilias*

In the mid twentieth century, scholars considered and eventually rejected[465] the claim of Johann Döllinger[466] and Adolf von Harnack[467] that Origen believed serious, post baptismal sins could not be forgiven.[468]

---

[464] *Hom. Luc.* 35.3–15 (SC 87:414–30).
[465] Rahner, "La doctrine," 73–79; Crouzel, *Origen*, 230.
[466] Döllinger, *Hippolytus*, 245–68.
[467] Harnack, *Lehrbuch*, 1, 448–49n1.
[468] Based primarily on *Or.* 28.10 (GCS 3:381).

In the process, two passages were highlighted in which Origen says that God "himself" punishes and heals people when the disciplinary efforts of ecclesiastical leaders and angelic agents fail. Scholars got the impression that, while petty sinners were corrected by angelic agents, extremely wicked sinners were disciplined by God himself.[469] Karl Rahner noticed that this conflicted with Origen's idea that grievous sin removes one farther and farther from God and that punishment often refers to the painful consequences of that removal. But Rahner noted that the vestiges of the Logos exist even in the souls of the worst sinners, and he suggested that, since their sin is an outrage against this Logos, they encounter it as an inner burning fire that can be considered the vengeance of God himself.[470] Rahner's solution is not compelling (or at least not complete), but the problem he identified is important for the present study; for if it is true that Origen distances God from the act of punishment through demonic agents, how could it be that God "himself" punishes the worst of sins? With this in mind, the two key passages are examined in the following text.

In Rufinus' translation of the first homily on Psalm 38 (= Ps 37 in LXX), Origen says that God uses Scripture, ecclesiastical authorities, and angelic "guardians and managers" (re: Gal 4.2)[471] to correct and rebuke fallen Christians. They must respond with humility, mortification of the flesh, and constructive terror of God's looming wrath. If, instead, they "have surpassed the limit of crimes," they will "bring upon themselves the vengeance of the divine hand, so to speak." They will be subjected to the "rage ... which is said to be God's." Origen compares this scenario to a household in which pedagogues reprimand children for light offences, but serious offences elicit "wrath," "torments," and even disownment from the head of the household (Lt: *paterfamilias*; Gk: οἰκοδεσπότης).[472] This is what Christians suffer who fall into darkness after having received "the knowledge of the truth" (re: Heb 10.26) and refusing to repent.[473]

In Origen's *Homilies on Jeremiah* (translated into Latin by Jerome), he notes that God "himself" (*ipse*) will repay "retribution" to Babylon (re: Jer 51.6 in LXX). For Origen, this means that God will not punish Babylon

---

[469] Poschmann, *Paenitentia*, 453; Bettencourt, *Doctrina*, 317; Rahner, "La doctrine," 59n50, 60–61n60, 81; Recheis, *Engel*, 80n31.
[470] Rahner, "La doctrine," 62, 83–84.
[471] Lt: *a procuratoribus et actoribus*; Gk: ἐπιτρόπους ... καὶ οἰκονόμους.
[472] *Hom. Ps. 37* 1.1 (SC 411:266–72).
[473] *Hom. Ps. 37* 1.6 (SC 411:296).

"through his ministers," as he is said to do in many Scripture passages. In those passages (e.g. Ps 78.49), God "makes use of (*usus est*) the evilest angels for retribution"; "perhaps" he also "makes a return to others not through bad [angels] but through good ones." According to Origen, these punitive angels are like the "servants" or "disciples" of a great doctor. When wound care and amputations are straightforward, they provide a cure themselves; but "incurable wounds and deep infections in necrotic flesh" require the skilled "hands of the master himself." This latter case is that of Babylon, which bears "the grave wounds of its own evil." That is why "God himself," the master physician, "hastens for retribution."[474] Origen finishes the homily with a warning to Christians. If they, like Babylon, reject the angelic ministers sent to heal them, these ministers will "give up hope for [their] souls" and "abandon" them. Such Christians will "plunge into worse things" and "die" outside the "hands of the holy angels who were appointed by God to care for [them]." As in the case of Babylon, the height of such people's sin, Origen says, will require a higher level of punishment, so God "inflicts his own judgement" upon them.[475]

The pastoral exhortation in both of the passages just considered is to respond to lighter discipline in order to avoid the coming judgment. Three manifestations of this scenario are given. First, Babylon ignored the correction of angelic ministers and so was punished (and healed) by God himself, either when Christ overturned pagan religion at the cross or at the consummation of the age.[476] Second, Israel ignored the pedagogy of the Law and the Prophets and even crucified Christ the great healer; therefore, she was punished by God himself, perhaps at the destruction of the Temple in AD 70 (re: Matt 23.34–38).[477] Third, Christians who fall into serious sin and ignore ecclesiastical and angelic exhortations to repentance and mortification will suffer the wrath of God himself. Origen might envision this on the last day, for he associates such a person's fate with that of the sinner in Hebrews 10.26–27, who suffers the "fearful expectation of judgment," although this last phrase is not quoted by Origen.[478] In addition, it is "in the day of the Lord" that the "destruction of the flesh" Origen advocates will "save" one (re: 1 Cor 5.5).[479] Finally,

---

[474] *Hom. Jer.* 50.2.6 (SC 238:350–52).
[475] *Hom. Jer.* 50.2.12 (SC 238:364–66).
[476] *Hom. Jer.* 50.2.11 (SC 238:358–60).
[477] *Hom. Jer.* 50.2.6 (SC 238:352).
[478] *Hom. Ps. 37* 1.1 and 1.6 (SC 411:266–72, 296).
[479] *Hom. Ps. 37* 1.2 (SC 411:278).

Origen warns against dying outside the hands of angelic caretakers, and he contrasts God's personal judgment of unrepentant sinners with his "paying back to the just person what his life in Christ deserves," which sound, again, like references to final judgment.[480]

Origen sees the entire panoply of earthly life as salvific pedagogy, and it makes sense for the last day to be an encounter with the divine Judge in which one answers for not having responded to this pedagogy. But Origen imagines a shadow of this scenario occurring at the Incarnation, when Christ surpasses the pedagogy of the Law, the Prophets, and the good and evil angels of the nations. The harsh discipline of evil angelic rulers was superseded when Christ "inherited" their domains and destroyed false knowledge[481] (note the connection with the overturning of pagan religion mentioned above). In addition, the unsuccessful efforts of good angelic rulers to stop the "creeping rottenness" of sin were superseded by the arrival of Christ the "master doctor" (*archiater*)[482] (wording almost identical to that of *Hom. Jer.* 50.2.6). Thus, it would not be surprising if Origen believed the Incarnation was the time when God himself judged and healed both Babylon, which had not responded to the pedagogy of its harsh angel, and Israel, which had rejected previous discipline.

But whether we are speaking about Christ's first or second coming, exactly what is meant by Origen's claim that God *himself* punishes? To answer this question, we could turn to Origen's general views of punishment after the Incarnation and after death. But these views (as we have seen) contain all the typical features of Origen's theodicy. In fact, some of these features appear in the same passages that mention "God himself" inflicting punishment. We have already seen Origen's statement that "rage" (*furorem*) is only "said to be God's,"[483] but there is a significant discussion of the matter in the first half of *Homilies on Jeremiah* 50.2. There, Origen says that "Babylon" represents Christians who, "although they at one time tasted of salvation" (re: Heb 6.4–6),[484] are "overwhelmed by excessive crimes."[485] Such people must "do penance" and submit to divine punishment, for it will improve and heal them. If they do not, they

---

[480] *Hom. Jer.* 50.2.12 (SC 238:366).
[481] *Princ.* 3.3.2–3 (Behr, 402–4); *Hom. Gen.* 9.3 (SC 7:248–50); *Hom. Luc.* 35.7 (SC 87:420); compare *Comm. Jo.* 13.410–15 (SC 222:258–62).
[482] *Hom. Luc.* 12.3–4 (SC 87:200–2); *Hom. Luc.* 13.1–3 (SC 87:206–8).
[483] *Hom. Ps. 37* 1.1 (SC 411:266).
[484] *Hom. Jer.* 50.2.3 (SC 238:344).
[485] *Hom. Jer.* 50.2.1 (SC 238:338).

will be "cast aside" (*abici*) meaning that God will cease to punish them. Indeed, this cessation of salvific torments might be called God's "great wrath" (re: Hos 4.14).[486]

Thus, Origen does not seem to have thought his statements about "God himself" punishing were inconsistent with his typical efforts to distance God from some aspects of punishment. If there is inconsistency, it nuances, but does not erase, the significance of Origen's typical efforts at theodicy.

3.10 Demons Are No Threat to God

The second-century Platonist Celsus objected to what some call the "dualist" element in Christian thought.[487] According to him, the Christian idea of Satan as "one who opposes God" and can thwart divine plans is "irreligious."[488] Demons are not evil rebels, as Christians think, for all superhuman beings "keep the law from the greatest God."[489] Thus, when Christians refuse to worship the cult gods (which Celsus takes to be demons who administer earthly things) they dishonor the servants of God and will suffer the consequences.

Origen agrees that the beings God has appointed to administer natural things are good, but he says that they are "angels" who do not want people to worship them. The cult "gods," on the other hand, are demons, who are always evil and should not be worshipped. These demons are responsible not for benefits but for disasters and plagues.[490] As we would expect, Origen claims that Satan and these demons were created good by God but then fell into sin;[491] but this does not really answer Celsus' objection that their ability to oppose God would threaten divine supremacy.

I believe Kurt Flasch is correct about Origen's answer to this, which is that Satan and his demons are subservient to God (Satan needed God's "permission" to attack Job); and divine providence puts even their evil activities to a good use.[492] As we have seen, God uses Satan to provide people with salutary struggles,[493] and plague-inflicting demons act with

---

[486] *Hom. Jer.* 50.2.4–5 (SC 238:344–48); compare *Hom. Exod.* 8.5 (SC 321:264–66); Rahner, "La doctrine," 68n88, 82–83; Koch, *Pronoia*, 134.
[487] Chadwick, *Origen*, 357n224; Pagels, *Origin*, 140.
[488] *Cels.* 6.42 (SC 147:278); compare *Cels.* 8.11 (SC 150:196–98); compare Plato, *Politicus* 269e–70a (Duke, 495–96); Russell, *Satan*, 129; Flasch, *Le Diable*, 77.
[489] *Cels.* 7.68 (SC 150:170).
[490] *Cels.* 8.31–32 (SC 150:242–44).
[491] *Cels.* 6.44 (SC 147:288); *Cels.* 7.69 (SC 150:174–76).
[492] Flasch, *Le Diable*, 78–79; *Cels.* 6.44 (SC 147:288).
[493] *Cels.* 8.70 (SC 150:336–38).

divine authority as God's "executioners."[494] Perhaps the Logos even considers demons appropriate to govern and chastise sinners in certain regions of the earth.[495] Thus, evil powers do not ultimately thwart God's will, and so they do not endanger monotheism and divine supremacy. Here we see that, for Origen – as for the Hebrew Prophets, the author of the Gospel of John, and Tertullian – the fact that God uses evil for good proves that it is no threat to him.

3.11 Conclusion

What is clear in the passages from *Against Celsus* cited at the end of Section 3.10 is implied in the other discussions of punishing demons earlier. As already noted, although the paradigms of "sending out," "handing over," and tax collecting serve to distance God from what is inconsistent with his nature, Origen consistently affirms that God directs punishing demons, or even appoints them as his ministers. There is no fear that such beings thwart God's plans, even if their actions are contrary to his will. In God's providence, the worst rebels are simply building blocks whose twisted shape makes them appropriate for certain places in the pedagogical structure of the cosmic house. There is no question of Origen having "turned Christianity into a highly dualistic religion."[496] As Origen says, the misfortunes caused by evil powers "are not done by God, and yet they are not [done] without God."[497]

Origen's idea that God providentially uses (but does not cause) evil choices is related to his view of the origin of free will and evil, for in both cases he tries to simultaneously uphold God's supremacy and goodness. According to Origen, the fact that God created free will means that nothing was created apart from him (God is supreme). At the same time, he is not responsible for the misuse of free will, so he did not create evil (God is good). Similarly, the idea that God uses evil choices for good affirms that no evil escapes his providence (God is supreme); and yet he is not responsible for the evil actions he uses (God is good). This vision of divine providence, including its exegetical manifestation, is a central but underappreciated pillar in Origen's theodicy. It goes beyond merely explaining why God allows evil to continue (*pace* Koch).

---

[494] *Cels.* 7.70 (SC 150:176); *Cels.* 8.31–32 (SC 150:242–44).
[495] *Cels.* 8.33 (SC 150:246).
[496] Kelly, *Satan*, 142–45.
[497] *Princ.* 3.2.7 (Behr, 398).

Origen based his vision, as this Element has shown, on a constellation of key Scripture passages and their surrounding traditions. As we have seen, his remarkable synthesis occasionally coincides in surprising ways with the conclusions of contemporary scholars of early Judaism and first-century Christianity: for example, Stokes's presentation of "the Satan" as God's "executioner" and Wasserman's vision of rebels who nonetheless serve in the administrative system of the divine King. What some will be surprised to see is that these ideas did not die out in the third century but rather found their most systematic expression.

Abbreviations

Translations of Greek and Latin texts, including the Septuagint and the New Testament, are my own. Translations of the Hebrew Bible are from the Revised Standard Version Catholic Edition. DeepL was used in the research process to more quickly assimilate scholarship in foreign languages that the author does not read rapidly, but it is never quoted.

Critical Editions

CCSL	Corpus christianorum: Series latina (Brepols, 1953–).
CSEL	Corpus scriptorum ecclesiasticorum latinorum (1866–).
GCS	Die griechischen christlichen Schriftsteller (De Gruyter, et al., 1897–)
LXX	Septuagint, using the text of Alfred Rahlfs and Robert Hanhart, 2nd ed. (Deutsche Bibelgesellschaft, 2006).
NT	New Testament, using the text of Barbara Aland, Kurt Aland, et al., 4th ed. (Deutsche Bibelgesellschaft, 1994).
OAP	Philonis Alexandrini opera quae supersunt. Edited by Leopold Cohn and Paul Wendland (Georg Reimer, 1896–1930).
PG	Patrologiae cursus completus: Series graeca. Edited by Jacques-Paul Migne (1857–66).
SC	Sources chrétiennes (Les éditions du Cerf, 1942–)

Titles of Ancient Texts

An.	*De anima*
Apol.	*Apologeticus*
Autol.	*Ad Autolycum*
Cels.	*Contra Celsum*
Comm. Isa.	*Commentarius in Isaiam*
Comm. Jo.	*Commentarii in evangelium Joannis*
Comm. Matt.	*Commentarium in evangelium Matthaei*
Comm. ser. Matt.	*Commentarium series in evangelium Matthaei*
Comm. Rom.	*Commentarii in Romanos*
Dial.	*Dialogus com Heraclide*
Ep. Afr.	*Epistula ad Africanum*
Ep. Greg.	*Epistula ad Gregorium Thaumaturgum*
Fr. Eph.	*Fragmenta ex comentariis in epistulam ad Ephesios*

Fr. Jer.	*Fragmenta in Jeremiam*
Fug.	*De fuga in persecutione*
Hist. eccl.	*Historia ecclesiastica*
Hom. Exod.	*Homiliae in Exodum*
Hom. Ezech.	*Homiliae in Ezechielem*
Hom. Gen.	*Homiliae in Genesim*
Hom. Isa.	*Homiliae in Isaiam*
Hom. Jer.	*Homiliae in Jeremiam*
Hom. Jes. Nav.	*In Jesu Nave homiliae*
Hom. Lev.	*Homiliae in Leviticum*
Hom. Luc.	*Homiliae in Lucam*
Hom. Num.	*Homiliae in Numeros*
Hom. Ps.	*Homiliae in Psalmos*
Idol.	*De idololatria*
Marc.	*Adversus Marcionem*
Op.	*Opera et dies*
Or.	*De oratione*
Orat. paneg.	*Oratio panegyrica in Origenem*
Orig. Hom. Cant.	*Homilae Origenis in Canticum canticorum Latine redditae*
Philoc.	*Philocalia*
Princ.	*De principiis*
Prov.	*De providentia*
Pud.	*De pudicitia*
4QD[a]	Damascus Document
1QM	War Scroll
1QS	Rule of the Community
Quest. rom.	*Quaestiones romanae*
Schol. Apoc.	*Scholia in Apocalypsem*
Sel. Gen.	*Selecta in Genesim*
Spect.	*De spectaculis*
Stoic. rep.	*De Stoicorum repugnantiis*

Titles of Secondary Literature

OD	*Origene: dizionario: la cultura, il persiero, le opere*, edited by Adele Monaci Castagno (Rome: Città nuova, 2000).
WHO	*Westminster Handbook to Origen*, edited by John Anthony McGuckin. Louisville, KY: Westminster John Knox, 2004.

Bibliography

Alcain, José Antonio. *Cautiverio y redencion del hombre en Origenes*. Ediciones Mensajero, 1973.

Alciati, R. "Il Cassiano greco di Panayotis Tzamalikos." *Rivista di storia del cristianesimo* 11 (2014): 451–78.

Alexandre, Monique. "La redécouverte d'Origène au XXe siècle." Pages 51–93 in *Les Pères de l'Église dans le monde d'aujourd'hui*. Edited by C. Badilta and C. Kannengeisser. Beauchesne, 2006.

Algra, Keimpe. "Stoics on Souls and Demons." Pages 71–96 in *Demons and the Devil in Ancient and Medieval Christianity*. Edited by Nienke Vos and Willemien Otten. Brill, 2011.

Allen, Garrick V. "The Reception of Scripture and Exegetical Resources in the Scholia in Apocalypsin (GA 2351)." Pages 141–63 in *Commentaries, Catenae and Biblical Tradition*. Edited by H. A. G. Houghton. Gorgias Press, 2016.

Barnes, Timothy David. *Tertullian: A Historical and Literary Study*. Oxford University Press, 1971.

Behr, John. *Origen: On First Principles*. 2 vols. Oxford University Press, 2017.

Benjamins, H. S. *Eingeordnete Freiheit*. Brill, 1994.

Bernoulli, Carl Albrecht. *Hieronymus und Gennadius: De viris inlustribus*. Mohr Siebeck, 1895.

Bettencourt, Stephanus Tavares. *Doctrina ascetica Origenis*. Libreria Vaticana, 1945.

Blowers, Paul M. "Rule of Faith." Pages 187–89 in *WHO*.

Bobzien, Susanne. *Determinism and Freedom in Stoic Philosophy*. Oxford University Press, 1998.

Bostock, Gerald. "Satan – Origen's Forgotten Doctrine." Pages 109–23 in *Origeniana Decima*. Edited by Sylwia Kaczmarek and Henryk Pietras. Peeters, 2011.

Bostock, Gerald. "The Sources of Origen's Doctrine of Pre-Existence." Pages 259–64 in *Origeniana Quarta*. Edited by Lothar Lies. Tyrolia, 1987.

Boulogne, Jacques. *Plutarque: Oeuvres morales*. Vol. 4. Le belles lettres, 2002.

Burns, Dylan M. *Did God Care? Providence, Dualism, and Will in Later Greek and Early Christian Philosophy*. Brill, 2020.

Casevitz, Michel. *Plutarque: Oeuvres Morales*. Vol. 15. Les belles lettres, 2004.
Chadwick, Henry. *Origen: Contra Celsum*. Cambridge University Press, 1965.
Chênevert, J. *L'Église dans le Commentaire d'Origène sur le Cantique des Cantiques*. Desclée de Brouwer, 1969.
Clark, Gillian. "Desires of the Hangman." Pages 137–46 in *Violence in Late Antiquity*. Edited by H. A. Drake. Routledge, 2016.
Cook, John Granger. "Envisioning the Panoply of the Roman Torturer." *Klio* 106/2 (2024): 647–70.
Crouzel, Henri. "Celse et Origène à propos des «démons»." Pages 331–55 in *Frontières terrestres, frontières célestes dans l'antiquité*. Edited by Béatrice Bakhouche. Presses universitaires de Perpignan, 2018.
Crouzel, Henri. "Diable et démons dans les homélies d'Origène." *Bulletin de Littérature Ecclésiastique* 95 (1994): 303–31.
Crouzel, Henri. "Le démoniaque dans l'oeuvre d'Origène." Pages 31–61 in *Figures du démoniaque, hier et aujourd'hui*. Edited by Michel Lagrée, et al. Facultés universitaires Saint-Louis, 1992.
Crouzel, Henri. *Origen: The Life and Thought of the First Great Theologian*. Translated by A. S. Worrall. Harper & Row, 1989.
Crouzel, Henri. *Origène et la «Connaissance Mystique»*. Desclée de Brouwer, 1961.
Daniélou, Jean. *Origène*. La Table Ronde, 1948.
DeCock, Miriam. "Origen's Sources of Exegetical Authority." *New Testament Studies* 70 (2024): 149–59.
de Lange, Nicholas. *Origen and the Jews*. Cambridge University Press, 1977.
de Lubac, Henri. *Exégèse Médiévale: Les Quartre sens de l'Écriture*. Vol. 1. Aubier, 1959.
de Lubac, Henri. *Histoire et esprit*. Aubier, 1950.
Döllinger, Johann. *Hippolytus und Kallistus*. G. J. Manz, 1853.
Dorival, Gilles, and Ron Naiweld. "Les interlocuteurs hébreux et juifs d'Origène à Alexandrie et à Césarée." Pages 121–38 in *Caesarea maritima e la scuola origeniana*. Edited by O. Andrei. Morcelliana, 2013.
Duke, E. A., et al. *Platonis opera*. Scriptorum classicorum bibliotheca Oxoniensis. Vol. 1. Clarendon, 1995.
Edwards, Mark. *The Problem of Evil in the Ancient World*. Cascade, 2023.
Edwards, Mark. *Origen Against Plato*. Ashgate, 2002.
Evans, Ernest. *Tertullian: Adversus Marcionem*. 2 vols. Oxford Early Christian Texts. Edited by Henry Chadwick. Oxford University Press, 1972.

Farrar, Thomas J. "The Intimate and Ultimate Adversary." *Journal of Early Christian Studies* 26 (2018): 517–46.

Farrar, Thomas J., and Guy J. Williams. "Diabolical Data: A Critical Inventory of New Testament Satanology." *Journal for the Study of the New Testament* 39 (2016): 40–71.

Fernández, Samuel. "'Passio Caritatis' According to Origen In Ezechielem Homiliae VI in the Light of DT 1,31." *Vigiliae Christianae* 60 (2006): 135–47.

Fernández, Samuel. *Cristo médico, según Orígenes*. Studia Ephemeridis Augustinianum, 1999.

Filoramo, Giovanni. *L'attesa della fine. Storia dello gnosticismo*. Laterza, 1983.

Flasch, Kurt. *Le Diable dans la pensée européenne*. Vrin, 2019.

Forsyth, Neil. *The Old Enemy*. Princeton University Press, 1987.

Fraade, Steven D. *The Damascus Document*. Oxford University Press, 2021.

Fuhrer, Therese, and Simone Adam, eds. *Aurelius Augustinus: Contra academicos, De beata vita, De ordine*. De Gruyter, 2017.

Gamble, Harry Y. *Books and Readers in the Early Church*. Yale University Press, 1995.

García Martínez, Florentio. *The Dead Sea Scrolls Translated*. Translated by Wilfred G. E. Watson. 2nd ed. Brill, 1996.

Garvie, A. F. *Aeschylus: Choephori*. Clarendon, 1986.

Gasparro, Sfameni Giulia. "Eguaglianza di natura e differenza di condizione dei λογικοί." Pages 301–19 in *Origeniana Quinta*. Edited by Robert J. Daly. Peeters, 1992.

Gentry, Peter J. "Origen's Hexapla." Pages 522–71 in *The Oxford Handbook of the Septuagint*. Edited by Alison G. Salvesen and Timothy Michael Law. Oxford University Press, 2021.

Girolami, M., ed. *L'Oriente in Occidente*. Morcelliana, 2014.

Givens, Terryl L. *When Souls Had Wings*. Oxford University Press, 2010.

Grant, Robert M. *Theolophilus of Antioch: Ad Autolycum*. Oxford University Press, 1970.

Gregg, J. A. F. "Documents: The Commentary of Origen upon the Epistle to the Ephesians." *Journal of Theological Studies* 3 (1902): 234–44.

Griffin, Carl W., and David L. Paulsen. "Augustine and the Corporeality of God." *Harvard Theological Review* 95 (2002): 97–118.

Gronewald, M. *Didymos der Blinde. Psalmenkommentar (Tura-Papyrus)*. Part 5: Kommentar zu Psalm 40–44, 4. Papyrologische Texte und Abhandlungen 12. Rudolf Habelt, 1970.

Gulaker, Cato. *Satan, the Heavenly Adversary of Man*. T&T Clark, 2021.
Hall, Claire. "Origen and Astrology." *Studia Patristica* 100 (2020): 113–21.
Hamori, Esther J. "The Early History of Satan: Before the satan Was Evil." Pages 82–87 in *Evil: A History*. Edited by Andrew P. Chignell. Oxford University Press, 2019.
Hamori, Esther J. "The Spirit of Falsehood." *The Catholic Biblical Quarterly* 72/1 (2010): 15–30.
Harl, Marguérite. "La mort salutaire du Pharaon selon Origène." *Studi e materiali di storia delle religioni* 38 (1967): 260–68.
Harl, Marguérite. "Recherches sur l'origénisme d'Origène: la 'satiété' (koros) de la contemplation comme motif de la chute des âmes." Studia Patristica 8. Akademie-Verlag, 1966.
Harl, Marguérite. *Origène et la fonction révélatrice du Verbe incarné*. Seuil, 1958.
Harnack, Adolph von. *Lehrbuch der Dogmengeschichte*. 3 vols. Vol. 1. Mohr, 1909.
Heine, Ronald E. "Origen." In Pages 188–203 in *The Routledge Companion to Early Christian Thought*. Edited by Jeffrey D. Bingham. Routledge, 2009.
Heine, Ronald E. *Origen: Commentary on the Gospel According to John Books 1–10*. FC 80. Catholic University of America Press, 1989.
James, Mark Randall. *Learning the Language of Scripture*. Brill, 2021.
Janssens, Y. "La thème de la fornication des anges." Pages 488–94 in *The Origins of Gnosticism*. Edited by Ugo Bianchi. Brill, 1967.
Junod, Éric. "Introduction." Pages 11–126 in *Origène: Philocalie 21–27 sur le libre arbitre. SC 226*. Les éditions du Cerf, 1976.
Kelly, Henry Ansgar. *Satan in the Bible, God's Minister of Justice*. Cascade, 2017.
Koch, Hal. *Pronoia und Paideusis*. De Gruyter, 1932.
Laeuchli, Samuel. "Origen's Interpretation of Judas Iscariot." *Church History* 22 (1953): 253–68.
Leemans, Johan. "Angels." In *WHO*.
Lindsay, W. M. *Isidori Hispalensis Episcopi: Etymologiarum sive Originum*. Vol. 1. Oxford University Press, 1911.
Malamis, Daniel. *The Orphic Hymns*. Brill, 2024.
Marcovich, Miroslav. *Athenagoras: Legatio pro Christianis*. De Gruyter, 1990.
Marek, Václav. *M. Tulli Ciceronis: Scripta quae manserunt omnia*. Vol. 16: *Orationes de lege agraria; Oratio pro C. Rabirio perduellionis reo*. Teubner, 1983.

Markschies, Christoph. "Origenes: Leben – Werke – Theologie – Wirkung." Pages 1–13 in *Origenes und sein Erbe*. De Gruyter, 2007.
Martens, Peter W. *Origen and Scripture*. Oxford University Press, 2012.
Martin, Dale B. "When Did Angels Become Demons?" *Journal of Biblical Literature* 129 (2010): 657–77.
Marra, Joseph. *Q. Septimii Tertulliani: De spectaculis, De fuga in persecutione, De pallio*. Paravia, 1954.
McGuckin, John Anthony. *Origen of Alexandria*. Lexington Books, 2022.
McGuckin, John Anthony. "Caesarea Maritima as Origen Knew It." Pages 3–25 in *Origeniana Quinta*. Edited by Robert J. Daly. Peeters, 1992.
McGuckin, John Anthony. "The Life of Origen." Pages 1–23 in *WHO*.
McGuckin, John Anthony. "The Scholarly Works of Origen." Pages 25–44 in *WHO*.
McIvor, J. S. *The Targum of Chronicles*. Liturgical, 1994.
Metzler, K. *Origenes, Werke mit deutscher Übersetzung*. Vol 1.1. De Gruyter, 2010.
Monaci Castagno, Adele. "Diavolo." Pages 114–18 in *DO*.
Monaci Castagno, Adele. "Origene e Ambrogio." Pages 165–93 in *Origeniana Octava*. Edited by Lorenzo Perrone. Peeters, 2003.
Monaci Castagno, Adele, ed. *Origene: dizionario: la cultura, il persiero, le opere*. Città nuova, 2000.
Monaci Castagno, Adele. *Il diavolo e i suoi angeli*. Nardini, 1996.
Monaci Castagno, Adele. "La demonologia cristiana fra secondo e terzo secolo." Pages 111–50 in *Il Demonio e i suoi complici*. Edited by Salvatore Pricoco. Rubbettino, 1995.
Monaci Castagno, Adele. "La demonologia origeniana fra speculazione filosofica e preoccupazioni pastorali." Pages 231–47 in *L'autunno del diavolo*. Edited by Eugenio Corsini and Eugenio Costa. Bompiani, 1990.
Monaci Castagno, Adele. *Origene predicatore e il suo pubblico*. Franco Angeli Libri, 1987.
Muehlberger, Ellen. *Angels in Late Ancient Christianity*. Oxford University Press, 2013.
Nautin, Pierre. *Origène*. Beauchesne, 1977.
Nemeshegyi, Peter. *La paternité de Dieu chez Origène*. Desclée, 1960.
Neuschäfer, Bernhard. *Origenes als Philologe*. 2 vols. Reinhardt, 1987.
Nickelsburg, George W. E. and James C. VanderKam. *1 Enoch: The Hermeneia Translation*. Fortress, 2012.

Niculescu, Michael Vlad. "Origen in Gethsemane." *Adamantius* 6 (2000): 8–25.

Niehoff, Maren R. "Origen's Commentary on Genesis as a Key to Genesis Rabbah." Pages 129–53 in *Genesis Rabbah in Text and Context*. Edited by S. Kattan Gribetz, et al. Mohr Siebeck, 2016.

Niehoff, Maren R. *Philo of Alexandria*. Yale University, 2018.

Norelli, Enrico. "Marcione e gli gnostici sul libero arbitrio, e la polemica di Origene." Pages 1–30 in *Il cuore indurito del Faraone*. Edited by Lorenzo Perrone. Marieti, 1992.

O'Leary, Joseph S. "Grace." Pages 114–17 in *WHO*.

O'Leary, Joseph S. "Judaism." Pages 135–38 in *WHO*.

Page, Sydney H. T. "Satan: God's Servant." *Journal of the Evangelical Theological Society* 50 (2007): 449–65.

Pagels, Elaine. "The Social History of Satan, Part II: Satan in the New Testament Gospels." *Journal of the American Academy of Religion* 62 (1994): 17–58.

Perrone, Lorenzo. *La preghiera secondo Origene: L'impossibilità donata*. Morcelliana, 2011.

Perrone, Lorenzo. "Libero arbitrio." Pages 237–43 in *OD*.

Perrone, Lorenzo. "Provvidenza." Pages 392–96 in *OD*.

Perrone, Lorenzo. "Looking at the World with the Eyes of God." *Studia Patristica* 131 (2024): 89–106.

Perrone, Lorenzo. "Origène." Pages 299–373 in *Découvrir les Pères de l'Église*. Edited by Marie-Anne Vannier. Perpigan, 2024.

Perrone, Lorenzo. "Un maître «très socratique»." Pages 141–63 in *Le lecteur collaboratif dans l'Antiquité tardive*. Edited by Sébastien Morlet and Antoine Paris. Les Éditions du Cerf, 2024.

Perrone, Lorenzo. "Origen's New *Homilies on the Psalms*." Pages 562–75 in *The Oxford Handbook of Origen*. Edited by Ronald E. Heine and Karen Jo Torjesen. Oxford University Press, 2022.

Perrone, Lorenzo. "Scrittura e cosmo nelle nuove Omelie di Origene sui Salmi." Pages 175–97 in *Meine Zunge ist mein Ruhm*. Edited by Alfons Fürst. Aschendorff, 2021.

Perrone, Lorenzo. "The Dating of the New Homilies on the Psalms in the Munich Codex: The Ultimate Origen?" *Proche-Orient Chrétien* 67 (2017): 243–51.

Perrone, Lorenzo. "Origen's 'Confessions'." *Studia Patristica* 56 (2013): 3–27.

Pettits, Jeffrey. "Transfiguration." Pages 204–5 in *WHO*.

Pohlenz, Max. *Die Stoa*. Vandenhoeck & Ruprecht, 1974.

Poschmann, Bernard. *Paenitentia secunda*. Hanstein, 1940.

Rahner, Karl. "La doctrine d'Origène sur la pénitence." *Recherches de Science Religieuse* 37 (1950): 47–97, 252–86, 422–56.

Recheis, P. Athanas. *Engel, Tod und Seelenreise*. Edizioni di storia e letteratura, 1958.

Rizzi, Marco. "La scuola di Origene tra le scuole di Cesarea e del mondo tardoantico." Pages 105–19 in *Caesarea Maritima e la scuola origeniana*. Edited by O. Andrei. Supplementi di Adamantius. Morcelliana, 2013.

Rogers, Rick. "Theophilus of Antioch." *Expository Times* 120 (2009): 214–24.

Roukema, Riemer. "Origen on the Origin of Sin." Pages 201–11 in *The Evil Inclination in Early Judaism and Christianity*. Edited by James K. Aitken, et al. Cambridge University Press, 2021.

Runia, D. T. "Philo of Alexandria." Pages 169–71 in *WHO*.

Runia, D. T. *Philo in Early Christian Literature*. Assen, 1993.

Russell, Jeffrey Burton. "The Historical Satan." Pages 41–48 in *The Satanism Scare*. Edited by James T. Richardson, et al. Routledge, 1991.

Russell, Jeffrey Burton. *Satan: The Early Christian Tradition*. Cornell University Press, 1981.

Scheck, Thomas P. *Origen: Commentary on the Epistle to the Romans Books 1–5*. Fathers of the Church 103. Catholic University of America Press, 2001.

Sgherri, Giuseppe. *Chiesa e Sinagoga nelle opere di Origene*. Vita e Pensiero, 1982.

Sheridan, Mark. "Scripture." Pages 197–201 in *WHO*.

Simonetti, Manlio. "Dio (Padre)." Pages 118–124 in *OD*.

Simonetti, Manlio. *Origene esegeta e la sua tradizione*. Morcelliana, 2004.

Simonetti, Manlio. *Lettera e/o allegoria*. Institutum Patristicum Augustinianum, 1985.

Simonetti, Manlio. "Due note sull'angelologia origeniana." *Rivista di cultura classica e medievale* 4 (1962): 165–208.

Solheid, John C. *Pedagogy of the Heart*. Brill, 2025.

Soon, Isaac T. *A Disabled Apostle: Impairment and Disability in the Letters of Paul*. Oxford University Press, 2023.

Stokes, Ryan E. *The Satan: How God's Executioner Became the Enemy*. Eerdmans, 2019.

Stroumsa, G. "The Incorporeality of God" *Religion* 13 (1983): 345–58.

Theißen, Gerd. "Monotheismus und Teufelsglaube." Pages 37–69 in *Demons and the Devil in Ancient and Medieval Christianity*. Edited by Nienke Vos and Willemien Otten. Brill, 2011.

Thompson, Fiona. "Demonology." Pages 85–86 in *WHO*.

Thornton, Dillon T. "Satan as Adversary and Ally in the Process of Ecclesial Discipline." *Tyndale Bulletin* 66 (2015): 137–51.

Thornton, Timothy C. G. "Satan: God's Agent for Punishing." *Expository Times* 83 (1972): 151–68.

Torjesen, Karen Jo. *Hermeneutical Procedure and Theological Method in Origen's Exegesis*. De Gruyter, 1986.

Trevijano Etcheverria, Ramon M. *En lucha contra las potestades*. Editorial ESET, 1968.

Trigg, Joseph Wilson. *Origen*. Routledge, 1998.

Trigg, Joseph Wilson. *Origen: The Bible and Philosophy in the Third-century Church*. John Knox, 1983.

Tzamalikos, Panayiotis. *An Ancient Commentary on the Book of Revelation*. Cambridge University Press, 2013.

Tzvetkova-Glaser, Anna. "Evil Is Not a Nature." Pages 180–89 in *Evil and the Devil*. Edited by Ida Fröhlich and Erkki Koskenniemi. Bloomsbury, 2013.

VanderKam, James C. *Jubilees: The Hermeneia Translation*. Fortress, 2020.

Vos, Nienke. "Introduction, Summary, Reflection." Pages 3–36 in *Demons and the Devil in Ancient and Medieval Christianity*. Edited by Nienke Vos and Willemien Otten. Brill, 2011.

Wasserman, Emma. *Apocalypse as Holy War: Divine Politics and Polemics in the Letters of Paul*. Yale University, 2018.

West, M. L. *Aeschyli Eumenides*. Teubner, 1991.

West, M. L. *Hesiod: Works & Days*. Clarendon, 1978.

Widdicombe, Peter. *The Fatherhood of God from Origen to Athanasius*. Oxford University Press, 2000.

Wright, Archie T. *Satan and the Problem of Evil*. Fortess, 2022.

Yli-Karjanmaa, Sami. *Reincarnation in Philo of Alexandria*. Society of Biblical Literature, 2015.

Acknowledgments

My deepest gratitude goes to Dan and Judith Heinze, my parents, friends, and patrons, without whom this Element would not have been written: it is dedicated to them Second, I will always treasure the many afternoons I spent dialoguing with Lorenzo Perrone during my sabbatical at the University of Bologna. This generous, humane, and consummate scholar commented on drafts at every stage of the project. Thanks also to Joseph Trigg, Andrea Villani, and John Solheid for their comments on the manuscript. It was Robin Darling Young whose encouragement and advice led me to Bologna, and Daniele Tripaldi and Andrea Villani who graciously welcomed me at the Department of Classical and Italian Philology. Finally, thanks to my wife and best friend, Hannah, and to our children, Vivian, Eliza, and Stratford, whose companionship and encouragement have made the journey worthwhile.

Cambridge Elements

Early Christian Literature

Garrick V. Allen
University of Glasgow

Garrick V. Allen (PhD St Andrews, 2015) is Professor of Divinity and Biblical Criticism at the University of Glasgow. He is the author of multiple articles and books on the New Testament, early Jewish and Christian literature, and ancient and medieval manuscript traditions, including *Manuscripts of the Book of Revelation: New Philology, Paratexts, Reception* (Oxford University Press, 2020) and *Words are Not Enough: Paratexts, Manuscripts, and the Real New Tesatament* (Eerdmans, 2024). He is the winner of the Manfred Lautenschlaeger Award for Theological Promise and the Paul J. Achetemeier Award for New Testament Scholarship.

About the Series

This series sets new research agendas for understanding early Christian literature, exploring the diversity of Christian literary practices through the contexts of ancient literary production, the forms of literature composed by early Christians, themes related to particular authors, and the languages in which these works were written.

Cambridge Elements

Early Christian Literature

Elements in the Series

The Author in Early Christian Literature
Chance E. Bonar

Maximos the Confessor: Androprimacy and Sexual Difference
Luis Josué Salés

Egeria: Theological and Ecclesial Knowledge Between Eastern and Western Traditions
Anni Maria Laato

The Pseudo-Clementine *Tradition: The Hermeneutics of Late-Ancient Sophistic Christianity*
Benjamin M. J. De Vos

Literate Workers and the Production of Early Christian Literature
Isaac T. Soon

Origen on Demonic Executioners and the Problem of Evil
Ky Heinze

A full series listing is available at: www.cambridge.org/EECL

For EU product safety concerns, contact us at Calle de José Abascal, 56–1°,
28003 Madrid, Spain or eugpsr@cambridge.org.

www.ingramcontent.com/pod-product-compliance
Lightning Source LLC
LaVergne TN
LVHW011854060526
838200LV00054B/4322